How Canon Got Its Flash Back

The Innovative Turnaround Tactics of Fujio Mitarai

How Canon
Got Its Flash Back

The Innovative Turnaround
Tactics of Fujio Mitarai

NIKKEI

Translated by
Mark Schreiber
and
Aaron Martin Cohen

John Wiley & Sons (Asia) Pte Ltd

Original work copyright © 2001 Nihon Keizai Shimbun, Inc.
Published by arrangement with Nihon Keizai Shimbun, Inc.

Published in 2004 by John Wiley & Sons (Asia) Pte Ltd
2 Clementi Loop, #02-01, Singapore 129809

Mark Schreiber and Aaron Martin Cohen, Adjunct Faculty Member, Empire State
College, State University of New York.

Other Wiley Editorial Offices

John Wiley & Sons, Inc., 111 River Street, Hoboken, NJ 07030, USA
John Wiley & Sons Ltd, The Atrium Southern gate, Chichester P019 8SQ, England
John Wiley & Sons (Canada) Ltd, 22 Worcester Road, Rexdale, Ontario M9W 1L1,
Canada
John Wiley & Sons Australia Ltd, 33 Park Road (PO Box 1226), Milton, Queensland
4064, Australia
Wiley-VCH, Pappelallee 3, 69469 Weinheim, Germany

Library of Congress Cataloging-in-Publication Data
0-470-82123-X

Typeset in 11/13 points, Stone Serif by Cepha Imaging Pvt, Ltd
Printed in Singapore by Saik Wah Press Pte Ltd
10 9 8 7 6 5 4 3 2 1

"Hats off to the authors for the thorough job they did in researching and organizing this book. The authors have expertly charted a course through the range of management reforms I have implemented since becoming CEO, providing context as well as a wealth of information on the company's history and traditions. The book provides readers with an insider's look at the company's transformation, presenting the road traveled thus far as well as the bright future that lies ahead for Canon."

Fujio Mitarai
President and CEO
Canon Inc.

Contents

Prologue

"Well, It's Finally Come to This."

GETTING OUT OF PCs

It was January 1996, at the Menlo Park, California, headquarters of Firepower, a fully owned Canon subsidiary engaged in the design and development of motherboards for personal computers. Yoichi Kawabata — Firepower's vice president — had just received orders from Canon headquarters to shut down operations. By July, the company had been sold to Motorola and the curtain descended on what Canon had once hoped would be the core of its personal computer business.

A decision from the top

The decision to pull out of Firepower had been made by Fujio Mitarai, who became CEO of Canon Inc. in September 1995. As one of his first acts, Mitarai had ordered Canon's total withdrawal from the personal computer business. By January 1997, the company had sold off its shares in software developer Next Computer to Apple Computer and shifted all matters related to its personal computer operations to its marketing subsidiary in Japan, Canon Sales. By October 1998,

Canon Sales had announced the halt to production of Canon-brand PCs.

Canon's computer operations had begun in 1974, when it launched sales of the Canonac office computer. In 1982, it had put its first personal computer, the AS-100, on the market. A year later, Canon Sales tied up with Apple Computer. and began sales of Apple PCs in Japan.

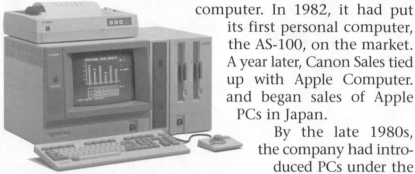

By the late 1980s, the company had introduced PCs under the NAVI and DX-20 brand names. In conjunction with IBM, it

The Canon AS-100 16-bit personal computer launched in 1982

had also marketed a PC with a built-in printer.

Excessive emphasis on PC operations

It was Canon's capital participation in Next Computer that led to the establishment of Firepower. Next Computer was the brainchild of Apple's legendary founder, Steve Jobs, who had devoted himself to the ambitious new venture following his departure from Apple. Job's plans failed to take off and, in 1993, Next's hardware and software divisions were split into two separate companies. Canon's management, while investing in Next Software, decided to take over the hardware division lock, stock and barrel, and in August 1993 the company was re-launched as Canon's fully owned subsidiary and renamed Firepower.

Canon's idea was to have Firepower serve as the core of rollback efforts for its PC business. Shortly after Firepower was established in January 1993, Canon vice president Hiroshi Tanaka half-threatened the newly appointed Kawabata by telling him he should not return to Japan until he had made a profit.

Kawabata had been one of 18 staff at Next Computer's hardware division who had been seconded from the parent company, and Firepower was positioned as Canon's most important project. As senior managing director Ichiro Endo, the group executive heading the Technology Management Headquarters, recalls, "We picked our most outstanding people to be assigned to this project."

If for no other reason than Next's failure, some took the view that the future would be difficult but Kawabata felt he stood a chance of success. In 1993, the so-called Wintel Alliance between Microsoft's Windows and Intel's microprocessors had only just begun its domination of the world PC market. At the time, however, IBM, Motorola and Apple were still in the running. On the front lines, the outcome of the battle was still uncertain.

Kawabata and his team had high expectations of the Power PC microprocessor chip being jointly developed by IBM and Motorola and were engaged in designing circuitry (referred to as "chip sets") for use with it. The Power PC was being billed as a rival to Intel products and, at the time, boasted the highest performance. In essence, the chip sets served as the heart of personal computers, designed to bolster the Power PC's performance when processing graphics and other functions. Firepower had planned to develop motherboards incorporating such chip sets, or computer CPUs, and supply them to computer manufacturers.

"We were hoping that if things went well, within three years we would offer company shares on the market," says Kawabata.

But developments in the PC industry were to dash Kawabata's hopes. The new Pentium CPU launched by Intel got the nod from PC manufacturers, and Intel achieved overwhelming dominance in microprocessors. The Power PC's backers, Firepower, succumbed to Wintel's supremacy.

Withdrawal

By the start of 1996, Firepower's problems could no longer be concealed. At that time, the Japanese contingent received top-secret orders from Canon headquarters to shut down operations. But there was a strong sentiment that to accept failure would mean that all the effort expended up to this point would have been in vain.

Instead of shutting down the company, Kawabata considered three possible actions: To keep the company intact but engage in extensive restructuring; to pull out the Japanese contingent but keep the company going; or to sell off the operation to another company.

Restructuring would have kept the company alive with some bloodletting, but was probably unlikely to happen. Mitarai, moreover, had issued an ultimatum to bring the Japanese contingent home. The game was up. As vice president, it was Kawabata's job to deliver the bad news to the other Japanese staff. To keep things a secret from the American staff, Kawabata summoned the members of his team to a nearby hotel where he could quietly deliver the bad news.

The Japanese staff who had been dispatched to Firepower were seasoned veterans. At the meeting, nearly all had requested to remain in the U.S. Many faced problems with their children's education. Assuming a long-term commitment to stay in the U.S., many had sent their children to local schools.

The staff reacted strongly to having to pull out midway. All had departed Japan for the U.S. with a sense of resignation, and after expending such great effort, everyone was opposed to capitulation — but none as much as Kawabata, who had been ordered not to come back until he had turned a profit. Some wept. "I felt like crying too," Kawabata says.

Unprofitable business not needed

But Kawabata was both realistic and persuasive and, one by one, the team members agreed to return to Japan. They began leaving in April 1996 and, at the end of June, Kawabata was the last to return to Japan. Around the time of the first Japanese departure, the U.S. staff was informed that the company was to be shut down. Motorola finally emerged as a buyer and many of the American staff were kept on by the new owner.

Before the order to shut down was sent out, the decision to terminate Firepower caused a furor in Canon headquarters, where Mitarai's decision was not easily accepted. As the weak member in Canon, the computer division, including the PC operations, had little success to show, having wavered between being Apple's representative in Japan and selling computers under its own brand. But within the company it was generally acknowledged that the PC was positioned as the center for data communications and information technology business.

Today, with PCs having become a commodity product, it's clear that this way of thinking was delusory. At the time, however, Canon was not the only company in the electronics and data business that still had high expectations of PCs.

As Firepower was the nucleus of Canon's PC operations at the time, shutting it down essentially meant Canon's withdrawal from the PC business. Subsequent events were to bear this out.

Because the decision came from Mitarai himself, the response to this shock, particularly from those in the technology-related divisions, was immense. Kawabata and, indeed, all the Japanese staff at Firepower understood that things were difficult but believed strongly that they could keep things going.

Canon had a tradition of developing its own technology. Its successful development of new technologies had led to the creation of new business, a pattern that had become a Canon specialty, and the force behind its growth. From its initial start in cameras, it had pursued this pattern with everything that followed — photocopiers, laser printers, Bubble Jet printers and semiconductor manufacturing equipment. It still pursues this system today. But obscured in the shadows of its more shining successes there were problems. Once the development of something was begun and recognized as an important technology, it would somehow be retained even after it became apparent that it was unlikely to be competitive or earn a profit. This was occurring not only at the research-and-development stage but also after reaching the stage of business operation. Canon, which subscribed to the Japanese style of emphasizing the importance of the efforts of those on the job, from the bottom up, had no means of putting an end to such operations. By his decision to withdraw from PC operations, Mitarai intended to wield the scalpel of reform throughout the organization.

Even for group executive Kunio Watanabe, head of Corporate Strategy & Development Headquarters, who reported directly to the president on reorganization and related matters, the decision to drop PC operations seemed to be abrupt. He believed that reform was necessary, and supported Mitarai's efforts, but was opposed to the closure.

"I was afraid that shutting down the operation might cause the president to lose his popularity, which in turn might wreck our efforts at reform," he says. The technical people in Canon still had a powerful voice within the company and he worried that any rebellion would have an adverse impact on future reforms.

"Looking at the way things happened, I have to apologize to Mitarai. At the time he was really alone and isolated," says Watanabe.

Mitarai explains: "When you ask for what purpose a company exists, you come up with such factors as a stable livelihood for its workers; return for investors; contribution to society; and surplus capital for the next investments. If you can't achieve these four, there's no purpose in existing. To achieve these, there has to be some sort of gain. Without advantage, none of the four can be realized. So first I emphasize to everyone in the company that we have to seek profit. A company is ordained, by definition, to be a profit-seeking entity. Consequently, I made the decision to halt all operations that weren't generating profits."

"One thing about the Japanese," he says, "They have a tendency to mistake methods for objectives. Then the methods become the objective and they risk their lives for it. I think that for them to assume this sort of risk for the company is a serious imposition. It bothers me to see people then devote their lives to a business that doesn't achieve earnings. I want to tell them to drop it, as fast as they can, and move forward with something else that will achieve those objectives. By making the choice to concentrate on things that will earn profits, we need to set down the roots of a culture that clearly delineates what methods to use."

Mitarai dealt firmly with those who resisted his decisions. "At the end, some of them came to me crying real tears," he says. But he kept pressing home his decision and, in the end, Canon sold Firepower.

SHEDDING FLCDs

Along with performing the coup de grace on personal computer operations, Mitarai made a succession of similar cuts to divest the company of other unprofitable business lines, some in technologies that were becoming obsolete. In June 1998, the production of electric typewriters was halted. In July 1999, production was likewise halted in optical cards and read/write devices. Among the sectors from which the company withdrew was flat-panel displays, a market it entered in 1984 and then exited in 1998, after suffering a loss of ¥100 billion. The following section discusses Canon's failed efforts in this market.

The dream of a wall-mounted TV

Flat-panel displays made of liquid crystal are thinner and lighter, and use less power, than conventional cathode ray displays. As such, they are the next wave in display devices. The technology would allow, for example, a TV set to be mounted on a wall. For this reason, major electronics manufacturers are engaged in a race to develop such displays.

The current leader in the field of liquid crystal display (LCD) is Sharp, which has concentrated its efforts on the development of display technology known as Thin Film Transistors (TFT).

Canon, a relative latecomer to LCDs, turned its attention to Ferroelectric Liquid Crystal Displays (FLCDs), a different technology from TFT. Canon chose this technology because it offers some advantages over TFTs, such as having no screen flicker. In 1984, the company obtained the basic patent rights on FLCDs from the University of Colorado and proceeded with research. In October 1991, it set up a separate FLCD division.

There was a major need for Canon to develop displays, which could be used in many of its devices. If Canon could develop a viable wall-mounted TV, for example, it could open a huge new market for the company. For this reason, the FLCD project generated tremendous expectations within the company.

A lonely battle

In May 1995, Canon launched its first commercial product, a 14.5-inch FLCD display. The product went on sale in May at the high price of ¥600,000 but the large screen size and high definition found buyers in high-end business clients, such as banks.

Canon's joy in producing this display was not to last. With a speed that the company had not foreseen, Sharp released products at a lower price but comparable in size and quality to those of Canon's. "Within a year, we had been beaten in terms of both performance and cost," says Katsumi Komiyama, a member of the development team who is now assistant director of the Display Development Center.

Meanwhile, in addition to Sharp, other major manufacturers in Japan and Taiwan had lined up behind the TFT technology. Competition was fierce but this expedited the development of TFT products. Canon, however, was the only major producer pushing the FLCD technology.

The development team decided that FLCDs could not compete head-on with TFT displays. Instead, the team turned its attention to markets other than personal computer displays, on which the TFT had focused. It pondered all possibilities, such as electronic paper that would substitute for conventional paper or large outdoor billboards.

"We considered everything in order to keep the project going," said Komiyama. In the end, however, no market emerged with demand comparable to that for PC monitors.

In autumn 1998, the development team made its last push. At an October exhibition at which technologies of various members of the Canon group were shown, the team showed a prototype of its latest FLCD, in the hope that it could garner support from Mitarai and the rest of the company. The strategy failed, as the display was still unable to reproduce images of the same quality and color as TFTs. Komiyama had a sense of resignation.

Soon after, Mitarai decided to pull the plug on FLCD production. When news that the product would be abandoned came down from the top, there was an outcry from the people around Komiyama. But in some ways he felt a sense of relief.

Fortuitously, a successor product called the surface-conduction electron-emitter displays (SED) came to the rescue. SED makes use of the same basic principle as a conventional TV tube. The technology was similar to those Canon had already developed for the inkjet printer, so the company felt it had an advantage in developing this technology.

Concurrent with his decision to pull the plug on the FLCD, Mitarai went ahead with plans to concentrate on SED flat-panel displays. Canon had begun basic research on the SED from 1986, and demonstrated a 10-inch color prototype in 1997. The SED had languished while work had progressed on the FLCD, but when the FLCD was killed, more resources could be put into SED development.

"Since we had the new work to do, we considered ourselves rather fortunate," says Komiyama.

CULTURE DEPENDENT ON PROPRIETARY TECHNOLOGY

The SED is another of Canon's original technologies. This time, however, the company chose not to go its own way. Mitarai approached Toshiba, which boasts a wealth of knowledge regarding television and personal computer displays, and proposed collaborative development. The two firms announced plans to engage in joint development in June 1999. This change from its usual policy of developing proprietary technology stirred controversy within Canon, but Mitarai announced a new approach.

"If you rely too much on your own, you'll fall behind. That was why the FLCD effort ended in failure," says Mitarai. "That doesn't mean that proprietary technology in itself is bad, but in the case of SEDs, for example, we ourselves have no technology for using it in television. If we had done things in the old style, we would have started to develop our own television technology. By the time we were on the verge of getting things right the situation could have completely changed. I want to speed things up, forming alliances or going through mergers and acquisitions, to get the things Canon doesn't have."

Komiyama now heads SED development. "I had to learn the lessons of our failure with FLCDs. First, rather than just developing a technology, we had to consider what the market needed," he says. The team at Canon engaged in SED development includes more than 100 with experience in developing FLCDs.

FISCAL HEALTH ATTESTS TO SUCCESS OF REFORMS

Canon has been reinventing itself since Mitarai became CEO in 1995. These reforms, beyond the changes in the product portfolio — such as getting out of the business of making personal computers and FLCDs — include many innovations in manufacturing. As described in subsequent chapters, the changes include, in particular, the shift from the conveyor-belt to the cell-assembly system. The figures tell the story of the impact these innovations have had on the company's fiscal health.

Over the period from 1991 to 1995, consolidated sales averaged ¥1.9 trillion. In the seven years from 1996 to 2003, sales rose 68% to ¥3.2 trillion. In terms of the product segments, in 1991, copiers accounted for ¥720 billion of revenues or 39% of the total. By 2003, although revenues from copiers had increased to approximately ¥1.1 trillion, as a percentage of total sales they had declined to 33%. During the seven-year period starting from 1996, the company achieved major growth in sales of inkjet printers and other computer peripherals. At ¥422 billion, peripherals accounted for 23% of sales in 1991; by 2003, revenues had risen to ¥1.1 trillion and 34% of total sales.

Profit levels also made major gains. Consolidated net profits in the 1991–1995 period averaged ¥39 billion. In 1996–2000, this had increased almost three times, to ¥105 billion. In 2003, consolidated net profit was ¥276 billion.

"Dropping out of personal computers, FLCDs and other unprofitable operations meant we lost more than ¥30 billion in sales. But it also erased a contribution of current losses coming to well over ¥10 billion," says Mitarai.

Radical surgery undoubtedly pushed up the company's profitability.

Canon's financial condition and operating efficiency also improved. The ratio of shareholder capital increased from 32% in 1991 to 59% by 2003.

A company's cash flow, which many consider the single most important indicator of business performance, improved dramatically. In 1991, Canon's free cash flow — the cash flow generated from business and investment activities — was around ¥54 billion; but by 2003 this had been turned around to ¥266 billion. The cash flow from sales in 1991 was positive, at ¥89 billion, but due to a negative ¥143 billion in cash flow from investment, the overall cash flow wound up in the red. By 2003, Canon's operating cash flow had ballooned to ¥466 billion.

From this cash flow generated by financial activities, we can readily see the degree to which Canon's reforms have succeeded. The total financial cash flow during the 1991–1995 period reached roughly ¥306 billion. The sales cash flow was not sufficient to cover that of investment funds, owing to a high dependency on outside procurement of funds.

The larger the financial cash flow, the greater the dependence on loans and other types of credit. Now we see that in the 1996–2000 period, total cash flow declined by approximately ¥451 billion. Canon, in other words, managed to reduce its borrowings by about ¥900 million per year. From 2000 to 2003, Canon managed to slash its long-term debt from ¥143 billion to ¥59 billion.

The cash-flow figures tell the real story of how Canon had harnessed its own considerable resources, generating the necessary cash flow from its businesses and delivering a good return on investment.

1

Prelude to a Reformation

A BRIEF CORPORATE HISTORY

The history of Canon can be divided into three distinct periods. The first was under Takeshi Mitarai, the charismatic first president. Next came the period during which Ryuzaburo Kaku headed the company. The third is the post-1995 era, when Fujio Mitarai assumed leadership of the entire group.

Takeshi Mitarai, first Canon president

An obstetrician becomes president

Takeshi Mitarai, a young obstetrician, and his friends Goro Yoshida, Saburo Uchida and Takeo Maeda had met for a beer, as they often did. It was 1933, and

The third-floor apartment in Roppongi, Tokyo, where Precision Optical Instruments Laboratory, the predecessor of today's Canon, was founded in 1933

on this particular evening the young men were engaged in a lively debate about Japan's place in the industrialized world. The four agreed that Japan's shipbuilding and textile industries were admired around the globe but that the country lacked precision industries such as camera-making. From this conversation arose Seiki Kogaku Kenkyujo — literally, "Precision Optical Laboratory," — which they set up in a three-story wood-frame building in the heart Tokyo's Roppongi district. Their dream: to produce a Japanese camera every bit as good as those made by the Germans. The following year, the group had produced a working prototype of Japan's very first 35mm camera with a focal-plane shutter. In 1937, when the company was reorganized as a maker of precision-optics equipment, employees were given lapel pins on which were combined a hawk and the company name, Seiki Kogaku. This year is now recognized as marking the start of the Canon company.

Not long afterwards, Japan fell into the war period. Uchida, the vice president who had been overseeing the administration of the company, was assigned by the Japanese government to a civil administration post in Singapore, which had been occupied by Japan in February 1942. At the time, Mitarai, who served as a company auditor, was operating an obstetrical clinic in Tokyo's Mejiro Ward and it was to him that the others turned to guide the company's fortunes.

"If things had been left as they were, we would have let down our investors and employees alike," Mitarai remarked. In 1942, he assumed the presidency.

At the war's end in August 1945, Allied Occupation troops were showing interest in buying cameras and were driving out to factories formerly operated by Seiki Kogaku Kogyo to buy them. Seeing this, Mitarai decided that cameras had a solid future and made the decision to tie the company's destiny to this product. In October 1945, he summoned back 56 of the workers who had been with the company when it was active to the Seiki Kogaku Kogyo plant in Meguro and relaunched the company as a camera-maker.

On the company's tenth anniversary in 1947, Mitarai changed the company's name to "Canon", arguing that "Seiki Kogaku" had no international appeal. The following year, the company name ceased to appear on cameras, being replaced instead by "Canon."

The birth of the Canon name

The Kwanon, Japan's first 35mm focal-plane shutter camera

When, in 1934, Goro Yoshida, one of the company's founders, made the first experimental camera, he gave it the name *Kwanon*, after the goddess of mercy in the Buddhist faith. The trademark he came up with showed an image of the

The logo that accompanied the Kwanon camera, derived from the Buddhist image of the Thousand-Armed Kannon

goddess, often depicted with a thousand hands, in a ring of flames, and the word *Kwanon* in stylized, flaming letters. Then, in June 1935, the company registered its first trademark.

The name "Canon" is the work of one of Yoshida's co-founders, Saburo Uchida. It seems that he wanted an image of a modern, high-quality camera, and this was more suitable than *Kwanon*. It seemed right for a camera, considering the pronunciation as "cannon" implies that cameras "shoot" pictures. Since the red-letter Canon logo was first designed in 1955, it has remained unchanged.

At the U.S. Camera Show held in San Francisco in 1949, the Canon II B model took first prize, one of the earliest recognitions of the increasing quality of Canon's technology. To raise its quality, Mitarai liked to hire engineers who were interested in developing quality products based on original technology.

At every opportunity, Mitarai emphasized the importance of what he called "the Three Selfs" — self-motivation, self-management and self-awareness — which were rooted in his three corporate maxims of meritocracy, health and neo-paternalism. The emphasis on good health no doubt stemmed from Mitarai's own medical background. The neo-paternalism concept stemmed from his view of family life as the basic unit of society, a view that, by extension, made Canon an extended family to its employees.

"The consistent theme of these corporate maxims is humanism," says Fujio Mitarai. "After all, the most important thing is people. This is not empty rhetoric. We took concrete steps such as the initiation of Japan's first five-day work week, as well as a system to help employees purchase their own homes."

In June 1960 Canon announced its plan to launch the Canonet, the company's first mass-produced camera. It was also Canon's first mid-range lens-shutter 35mm camera and featured an electronic light meter that automatically set the aperture. And, at ¥19,800, the Canonet was considerably cheaper than all the focal-plane shutter models that had preceded it.

At the time, the camera industry coordinated matters of interest by a means of a council headed by directors representing the manufacturers, wholesalers and retailers. The directors met each spring and autumn to discuss the appropriate pricing of new camera models. Canon chose to buck this system by pricing its new model at less than ¥20,000, which led to complaints that this aggressive pricing would disrupt the marketplace. One magazine went so far as to publish a special feature entitled, "Canonet — Drop Dead!" Yet the controversy had the advantage of giving the Canonet nationwide attention. The day the camera went on sale, it completely sold out.

Cameras in the right hand, business machines in the left

Rivalry between Canon, Nikon and other firms had the effect of giving Japan's camera industry a lead over its German counterpart. But dependency on a single product line was perceived as a weakness by Takeshi Mitarai and, in 1962, he decided to issue guidelines for expansion into other areas. His target sector was office equipment, including copiers. In 1964, Canon launched the world's first 10-key electronic calculator. A year later it entered the copier field.

In a speech in 1967, the year when the company would observe its 30th anniversary, Mitarai coined an expression still used to describe the basis for Canon's business today: "Cameras in our right hand and business machines in our left." On the basis of these two businesses, he vowed to push sales beyond ¥30 billion.

Behind the plan to make copiers was another aim: business operations that would be sustained by sales of consumable items. In the photography business, film manufacturers made more money than the camera-makers.

"In selling cameras, aren't we contributing to film-makers' profits? Thus if we enter the copier business, we can also generate business by selling toner cartridges and paper," Mitarai reasoned.

One of the biggest stumbling blocks in the way of Canon's move into this market was the fact that Xerox held most of the patents for plain-paper copiers. Disregarding this, Mitarai plunged ahead and ordered staff to proceed with development. In 1968, Canon researchers succeeded in developing a proprietary system for plain-paper copiers through covering the photoreceptor with a dielectric film. Canon's first move into diversification had come in 1964, when it introduced the Canola 130, the world's first 10-key desktop calculator. By the 1970s, Casio and Sharp had entered the market and competition in pricing and in developments such as miniaturization had become intense. Then, in October 1973, the Arab oil-producing states announced an export embargo, causing Japan to plunge into a recession arising from its high dependence on imported oil.

The following spring, problems arose from a shortage of components for the company's low-priced calculators and gave many consumers the impression that all Canon calculators were defective. In the ensuing ruckus, almost one-third of its sales channels chose to drop Canon models, creating a huge surplus of finished goods. In the first half of fiscal 1975, the company — for the first time in its history — suffered a loss and decided not to pay a dividend. Calculator sales, which had reached ¥93 billion in the second half of 1974, dropped to ¥63 billion in the first half of 1975.

In 1974, Takeshi Mitarai was replaced as president of the company by Takeo Maeda. Ryuzaburo Kaku was promoted from his position as director jointly responsible for the

Finance and Accounting Division to managing director, joining Maeda and the other top executives in formulating a new
corporate vision that would deal with the matter of earnings
by making each business division in the company responsible for justifying its existence by generating its own profit.

At the start of 1976, Canon announced its concept of corporate excellence, which called for the adoption of many
changes. These included the following: that the company
would establish and promote its principles in an open and
public manner; that ties within the Canon group would be
reinforced; that greater emphasis would be placed on the
ability to develop original technology; that more effort would
be made in developing human resources; and that efforts
would be made to implement company-wide improvements.
Kaku was entrusted with overseeing these changes.

In May 1977, however, Maeda died of lung cancer. On
June 2, the day after his funeral, Mitarai selected Kaku, then
51, as the new president. The man who had drafted the concept for corporate excellence was thus suddenly elevated to
the company's top position.

Business divisions as profit centers: The pros and cons

During his tenure as president, Kaku notched Canon's ratio
of R&D expenditures way up, from 5% of sales to 10%. As
would be expected from this increase, he also built up the
R&D staff. Results? The new system ushered in a bottom-up
management by engineers, who succeeded in developing
new products. The result was a rapid expansion of Canon's
operations — from copiers to printers, facsimiles, computers
and other products.

In 1987, the number of U.S. patents applied for by Canon
surpassed the number for IBM, making it the top company
filing in the United States. A look at the trend of the number
of patent applications shows a remarkable correlation
between the number of those applications and the company's consolidated business performance. The emphasis on
converting technology into intellectual-property rights, as a

means for spurring corporate growth, can be said to be one of Kaku's creations.

The first half of the 1980s stood out as a period of rapid growth. But from the mid-1980s, the company's momentum began to decline. Then came an agreement among the industrialized countries to weaken the value of the dollar, under the 1985 Plaza Accord, which led to the soaring value of the Japanese yen. The stronger yen made Japanese exports more expensive overseas, crimping sales. Setting up factories overseas in order to cope with this, for example, would have required each division to set up its own factory operations, even within the same country — something akin to subsidiaries spawning their own subsidiaries.

Canon's failure to shut down unprofitable operations was causing the company to hemorrhage cash. Thus came some hard decisions to shut down various operations. The effect of these decisions would not favor the development of new business. Canon was still waiting for a hit product that would turn things around. But it did not materialize. The flaws in the division-based system became increasingly evident and it appeared that the company was heading for a crash.

Arrival of an American-bred "bear"

Fujio Mitarai, nephew of Canon's first president, Takeshi Mitarai, was born in the town of Kamae, Oita Prefecture, in 1935. Blessed with good natural surroundings, Kamae's population supported itself through agriculture and fishing.

Fujio's father, Nobuo Mitarai, operated his own medical clinic and three elder brothers and one elder sister were also physicians. As Takeshi, Nobuo's younger brother, was also an obstetrician, the Mitarai clan could truly be called a medical family. Fujio was allowed much freedom in his upbringing and had a reputation among his peers as a *gaki-daisho* or leader of the pack. Fujio graduated from Tokyo's Chuo University Faculty of Law in 1961 and entered Canon the same year. "I didn't have any prospect in mind other than this job and was somehow also thinking I wanted to go abroad," Mitarai recounts. "At any rate, I felt that at least my elderly father would stop worrying about my career if I joined a good company like Canon, so I made the decision to join." In 1966, Mitarai was assigned to Canon's American subsidiary in New York. By 1979, he had become its president.

By the time Fujio returned to company headquarters in 1989, he had spent 23 years in the United States. Thus, his business education was based to a large extent on American practices. While Mitarai is still certainly very supportive of Japanese practices, he also demonstrates a dry, rational, U.S. way of thinking.

"Canon opened a New York office in 1955. It was selling products locally through Bell and Howell, but since they had their own camera lineup they didn't sell many of ours. Our rival Nikon, by contrast, was doing better in the U.S. market. Thus, around 1965 the sentiment arose to make another assault on the U.S. market. The contract with Bell and Howell was due to run out in December 1966, and in the beginning of 1967 our new subsidiary was launched, which is when I arrived," says Mitarai.

"There had been plans to assign more Japanese staff after me but the Japanese economy was in a slump and this plan was scrapped. Then the Bell and Howell contract was extended for another six years. About a hundred of my colleagues had seen me off at Tokyo's Haneda airport and it would have been shameful to return home without having accomplished anything. I made an all-out effort to research the camera market. Six years went by like this and then, in 1972, the Bell and Howell contract finally ran out. By then, Canon had recovered its vitality and, as general manager in charge of camera sales, I launched sales operations in the U.S. Afterwards, I took pride in having developed camera sales in the U.S.," says Mitarai.

A business lesson from the IRS

Mitarai continues: "I learned the importance of pursuing profits after being transferred to Canon U.S.A., which had only just been established. The year was 1966 and I was in

Fujio Mitarai, August 1966, soon after his arrival in New York

charge of accounting as we were preparing for our first settlement of accounts. We had posted $3 million in sales but failed to make any profit. But, to show a profit on my books, I requested permission from our business partners to delay payment until the start of the next accounting period. As a result, we were able to record $6,000 profit — on paper, if not in reality. A few months later someone from the U.S. Internal Revenue Service came to pay us a visit. Because our profits had been so small in relation to sales, we were under suspicion of having evaded paying taxes. Upon further inspection, however, it was discovered that we had failed to even turn a profit. In light of the situation, the tax officer told me I should collect all of my accounts receivable, put the money in a fixed-deposit account and go back home. He explained that by doing so, I could earn 5% interest without having to work. It was then that it hit me: if we were not able to achieve a profit that exceeded the interest rate, there was no reason to be in business.

This taught me a valuable lesson. In the U.S., unless your profit surpasses the rate of interest, there was no point in doing business. Since then, I've always taken it to heart to seek a profit. I thank the Internal Revenue Service for giving me my first important lesson in the American way of doing business."

Mitarai's philosophy of pursuing profit developed during his time in the U.S. Because Mitarai went to the U.S. at a fairly young age, he had a chance to learn these lessons before he became too wedded to the Japanese corporate practices, as had been the case with many of his peers. He also formed friendships with people on the front lines of

Jack Welch, former CEO of General Electric, with Fujio Mitarai

management; people like Jack Welch, later the CEO of General Electric, whom he met through dealings in plastic. They still get together whenever Welch visits Japan. This put Mitarai in a unique situation among Japanese management.

One of but a few

Looking at the parent company's situation from his American perspective, Mitarai felt exasperated. Then came orders from Kaku for him to return to Japan. Kaku resigned from the presidency, to be replaced by Keizo Yamaji. Contrary to the usual way of doing things, Mitarai was brought onto the board of directors as a senior managing director responsible for the administrative side of the company. In a technology-driven company with so many engineers, he found himself in something of a backwater in the company.

Kaku and Mitarai had come to an understanding on this. Kaku had often visited Mitarai in the U.S. and the two had always met when Mitarai visited Tokyo. Kaku and Mitarai had many frank talks.

Yamaji had risen from the ranks of the engineers, and of the six directors with representative power, Kaku was the only one with an administrative background. It made sense to add one more. Mitarai supposes this was the basis for Kaku's decision.

In March 1989, when Kaku became chairman and Yamaji was named president, Mitarai returned to company headquarters and assumed the position of senior managing director with responsibility for administration.

Mitarai could be tough in criticizing his subordinates. Some regarded him as being too critical but few hated him. Mostly, his style was likened to that of a gruff but good-natured bear.

Financial matters — the first breakthrough

Mitarai's years in the U.S. had led him to believe that Canon was overly dependent on its decentralized operations. It was only when he had returned to Japan and begun working there that he realized there were more problems than he had first anticipated. First, in the fiscal and accounting departments where he had direct responsibility, the most fundamental job of producing a budget was not being accomplished. The annual budget was being produced from the accumulation of requests submitted by each division. Given that the budget is the allocation of the company's resources, it was top management who should have been drawing it up.

Taking control of the budget

Because the divisions were akin to companies within the company, there was no means by which Headquarters could oppose the budget requests issued by the all-powerful divisions. Some divisions, for example, also shifted unsold inventories onto subsidiaries, which artificially boosted their results but did nothing to help the company overall.

As a technology-driven company, there was also a tendency at Canon to under-emphasize financial matters. In the absence of a genuine corporate planning function that governed the entire company, the accounting department, whose job it was to scrutinize the entire company and make necessary adjustments, had become no more than a center for shuffling paper.

"What's the matter with this company? We've got no budget planning system in force at all. What's the accounting department doing?" asked Mitarai of Toshizo Tanaka, then general manager of the Accounting Division and now group executive for the Finance & Accounting Headquarters. Tanaka had also been assigned to the U.S. and had worked with Mitarai before. The two enjoyed a close relationship. "We didn't just work together. When we were both single, there were times we'd go out and have fun all night," says Tanaka.

Looking at Canon's earnings structure at the time, office equipment had accounted for about 80% of total revenues and the company also depended on it for most of its profits. Cameras and optical equipment were generating losses.

Mitarai had to wrest back control of the budget from the business divisions. He set up his office adjacent to the accounting division — next to the battlefront, so to speak — and, in consultation with Tanaka, made plans to take back control of the budget.

His strategy was to introduce a system under which staff from headquarters and accounting departments were assigned to work in the divisions. This was necessary because, at the time, the divisions not only had the power to generate their own budgets, they also controlled internal personnel affairs.

"At the time, since we were getting no advance information regarding budget and other matters, we had no idea what to expect until each budget request arrived from the division," says Tanaka. So collecting information that would give a picture of what was going on became the first task of the managers sent to work in each division.

Not surprisingly, there was vehement opposition to the new moves. The new arrivals were regarded as spies and not invited to internal division meetings. Eventually, the division heads realized that the staff had not been assigned simply to collect information but were in a position to smooth relations between the divisions and headquarters, which helped them gain acceptance.

In March 1993, Hajime Mitarai became president. Hajime was the oldest son of Canon's first president, Takeshi Mitarai. After obtaining his doctorate in electrical engineering from Stanford University, Hajime had worked in electronics research at American companies. He had not planned to return to Japan but when Canon began to diversify from cameras into the electronics field, the company needed people with his background and he was strongly urged to join the company.

After Hajime joined Canon he worked in R&D and was involved in the development of a number of areas that subsequently became new product lines. While head of the research lab, he also introduced a freer working environment by adopting such methods as the U.S.-style flexible work hours.

When Hajime Mitarai became president, Fujio was promoted to executive vice president. He was eager to apply the methods he had used in streamlining the collection of data for the budget across the corporation. Hajime, the technician, was something of a straight arrow and gaining his approval for anything always took time. Fujio was finding that the authority held by the man at the top and that held by the No. 2 man were completely different. As vice president, however, he was appointed to chair the new Business Development Committee and started to think of ways to eliminate unprofitable new operations. He bided his time, if a little impatiently.

The turning point that led to major changes at Canon came about in a manner that no one had anticipated. On August 31, 1995, Hajime Mitarai died suddenly of interstitial pneumonia, at age 56. He had fallen ill in late June and had taken medical leave. But in July he returned to work and appeared to be well on the road to recovery; but his good health lasted only a month.

The news came as a shock. On the evening of Hajime's passing, chairman Ryuzaburo Kaku headed discussions on a successor and a confidential decision was made to appoint Fujio Mitarai as Hajime's successor. On September 1, an emergency meeting of directors was convened and Mitarai's appointment was officially approved and announced to the public.

"I was older, at 59, than Hajime, and never expected to become president because of my age," Fujio recalls. At the time, however, Fujio was in Canon's No. 2 slot and his succession was not wholly unnatural. On September 1, Kaku and Mitarai held a joint press conference in Tokyo, the gist of which follows.

Kaku: Our former president passed away suddenly. Avoiding delay in appointing his successor, the board of directors has made its decision today. The main factor in our decision to appoint Fujio as president and CEO of Canon is his strong leadership qualities. He succeeded in developing our U.S. subsidiary from a company with sales of a few million dollars into a $2.6-billion company. In the future, companies will need younger blood. It would have been better to have a person just over 50, but no experienced person of that age group was available, so we turned to Fujio Mitarai.

Mitarai: While I have yet to get over the loss of our president, I would like to stress that while continuing to pursue the corporate maxim based on the concept of *kyosei* ["living and working together for the common good"], I would like to pursue a global approach. In order to overcome the difficulties we face in these times, I intend to pursue management that focuses on high added value. As I am something of a fatalist, all I can do is to pledge to do my best in every possible environment, no matter what kind of situation I confront.

At the start of his first conference as president, Mitarai outlined his approach by paraphrasing the aphorism made famous by Chinese leader Deng Xiaoping: "As long as the cat manages to turn a profit, it doesn't matter if it's black or white."

He added: "Unprofitable divisions should be closed. On the other hand, it's fine if divisions can boost business by selling our products for resale under other companies' brands. The purpose of a company is to make profits."

Nor did he limit such pronouncements to executive conferences; essentially the same remarks were made whenever he exchanged words with directors and regular staff. "Managers should not be like flounders that can only see upwards. We need to look down from the top. First, we must set the right objectives. At that time, we should absolutely not ask subordinates for their opinion. Subordinates' opinions are needed only to refine the battle techniques. Then when we move toward implementation, take the lead and set an example for others. Unless you do things that way, you won't know how much progress you've really made," he says.

Mitarai is known for making top-down statements but these are not necessarily intended to be just orders from the president. They also include advice for managers to set objectives for themselves and take the leadership in their own part of the organization.

"The most important thing in Canon is not technology. It is money," says Mitarai. Canon is a company driven by engineers. There are about 2,000 staff who are at the level of manager or above; of these, about 80% are graduates of engineering schools. Engineers are said to dislike conspicuous discussions regarding money but a company without profits can't survive, regardless of its technology.

The decisive battle for Canon U.S.A.

In 1980, Canon launched sales of a new photocopier in the United States. The model was smaller and better than its predecessors. The model, unfortunately, developed problems. Static electricity in parts of the U.S. with low humidity caused the machines to generate "ghost" images. Canon was soon flooded with complaints from areas where the problem occurred. Irate dealers insisted that they could not sell the models they had been given.

In the midst of these problems, a trade show was being held in Las Vegas. Mitarai, president of Canon U.S.A. at the time, was to deliver the keynote speech at the event, where many of the dealers would be present. While understandably nervous about how the dealers would receive him, Mitarai decided he had to go ahead with the presentation.

Some 5,000 participants gathered at the meeting. As Mitarai commenced his speech, muttering could be heard in the audience. By the end of his speech, the hall had still not quieted down, and Mitarai, with a sinking feeling, descended from the podium. Then suddenly one of the participants, Jerry Banfi, president of DupliFax, a copier company in Philadelphia, took the microphone unannounced and stood up for Mitarai. In areas such as Philadelphia, where the air is relatively humid, the new copiers were apparently performing well and enjoying strong sales.

Mitarai, thinking this was his second chance, grabbed the microphone and for the next half hour delivered an emotional impromptu address. "Our fate is inseparable from the fates of our dealers," he said. "Unless dealers prosper, we won't prosper either. Sometimes a manufacturer has setbacks, but these will be fixed. We are working hard on improvements. Please trust me." The audience responded to Mitarai's appeal with applause. Anyone who had looked closely at Mitarai when he left the meeting would have seen that he was drenched with sweat. "That meeting was crucial for us," Mitarai recalls. "It raised the dealers' morale and boosted our ability to make sales."

Haruo Murase, another Canon U.S.A. alumnus and now president of the company's Japanese marketing arm, Canon Sales, was in the audience when Mitarai made his speech. "At first I thought anything could happen," he recalls. "But the spontaneous presentation seemed to turn the tide and I was astonished how Mitarai's ad lib remarks changed the dealers' attitude. Under pressure, he can be exceptionally persuasive."

Responding to the critics

Canon Inc. president and CEO, Fujio Mitarai

When Fujio Mitarai was appointed president and CEO of Canon Inc., he was the third member of his family to have reached this position, a fact that certain members of the media were quick to criticize. There were cynical references to *taisei hokan*, the term referring to imperial rule. Mitarai reacted strongly to the implications of nepotism.

"The reason Canon is regarded as a good

company is because of its merit-based corporate system. I made it to the head of the company without any help from belonging to the Mitarai family. It makes me mad when people say that Canon is a family business," says Mitarai. He is also quick to point out that none of his children work at Canon.

Even now Fujio Mitarai still bristles when the subject of Canon being a family business is raised. "When Hajime Mitarai joined the company, it was at Canon's request," he says. "They wanted engineers for diversification into electronics. But at the time, even though we had electrical engineers, we couldn't get electronics engineers to join. So we resorted to this."

Mitarai's career at Canon evokes comparisons with Kunio Takeda, president of Takeda Pharmaceutical Industries. Like Canon, Takeda is closely associated with the family that founded the company but, from the beginning, it has never been bound to having a family member serve as its president. After Kunio's older brother died while jogging, a non-family member served as president before Kunio was promoted to the position.

"I'm just a hanger-on," Kunio has remarked wryly. Like Mitarai, Kunio had spent an extended period at the company's U.S. subsidiary. And like Mitarai, once at the company helm, Kunio Takeda initiated corporate reforms at a dizzying pace. He had to neutralize internal resistance but continues to incorporate new methods, such as the adoption of a merit-based personnel system. The company's business performance has improved and, after dealing with the challenge of a lawsuit brought against a joint venture Takeda had in the United States, has proceeded with internationalization of its R&D activities.

Efforts to revitalize a business are certain to result in resistance from vested interests. It is often difficult, if not impossible, for a Japanese president to overcome this resistance. Having come up through the ranks themselves, such individuals are, more often than not, more likely to support the old way of doing things. Unless they are endowed with a tremendous sense of mission, they are unlikely to implement major reforms. Furthermore, any person from the founding family who has been groomed for succession, even if contending with inertia, will have to deal with the same types of tensions between the old and the new. They are bound by all kinds of fetters. It seems somehow appropriate that reformers such as Mitarai and Takeda, while members of the founding family on the one hand, developed their business careers apart from their corporate centers of power. In almost all of Japan's companies, even when there are people who are capable of doing specific jobs, there are few professional managers who can take charge of an entire organization. If such a person exists, it doesn't matter whether he originates from the founding family or comes up through the ranks. If it turns out that a member of the founding family has charisma, that certainly could be an advantage.

As Canon continued to post improved business performance, grumbles over Mitarai's family ties diminished and have now virtually vanished.

Mitarai's other chief concern was his relationship with Kaku. Just as Kaku had rejected certain aspects of Takeshi Mitarai's way of doing things, Fujio disagreed with some facets of Kaku's approach. However, the two were kindred spirits as Kaku, like Fujio, was one of the few Canon directors with an administrative background, and Fujio also felt indebted to Kaku for calling him back from an overseas post and making him senior managing director. After Fujio took over as president, he was always careful to seek Kaku's opinion before undertaking any moves to undo the business division system that Kaku had put in place. In response, Kaku told him, "Just keep on doing as you see fit."

Kaku passed away on June 23, 2001. At a company memorial service, Mitarai delivered the eulogy. "By continuing to pursue the spirit of *kyosei* among the world's people, as espoused by Kaku," he said, "Canon has come to be a respected brand."

Long-term corporate planning: The signal fire

While from the outset Mitarai took every opportunity to hammer home the need for reform, he felt that his vision needed to be expressed in a form that would be easily understood, such as through a long-term business plan. In a policy statement delivered as part of the traditional new year's address to the employees, Mitarai unveiled his long-term vision. During his first three months in office, he had worked out a framework embodying such standards as enhancing cash-flow management to improve the bottom line.

But Mitarai had only one month to prepare his announcement. Because the divisions still operated with a fairly high degree of autonomy, the Corporate Planning Headquarters, now the Corporate Strategy & Development Headquarters, was not able to grasp many of the problems within the company.

"There were still a lot of rough edges," says Kunio Watanabe, group executive of Corporate Strategy & Development Headquarters. "But with the idea of making improvements throughout the group, including overseas, he began putting together the framework for the concept of what we call an 'excellent global company'. At the same time, he was getting ready to deal with the problem posed by the excesses of the division-centric system."

After he had sewn the seeds of these new concepts in his new year's address, Mitarai traveled extensively to ensure that they took root. During January 1996, he visited every Canon office and factory in Japan, discussing his views on consolidated management and the best ways of going about things. Afterwards, he made five or six trips a year to expand on his vision. He also made certain to visit overseas offices at least once a year for direct talks with local executives and managers.

While the long-term corporate plan signaled where reforms were headed, Mitarai turned to the financial changes he had been involved with during his tenure as senior managing director and vice president. His long-term business plan included the introduction of a consolidated business performance system by division.

This was a method for calculating business performance by reviewing the entire business flow, from development and production to sales and after-sales service, by division. Up to then, all each division had to do was develop the products, produce them and supply them to the sales companies. If sales were unfavorable and inventory accumulated, that was the sales companies' problem.

Under the new system, the division's performance would no longer be appraised merely on the basis of developing lots of products and manufacturing them. Conversely, if a sales company was left with unsold merchandise, this was treated as inventory that had reverted back to the entire division. The divisions were obliged to improve their understanding of markets and the top management of each division was required to monitor production, sales and service according to a single standard. This consolidated approach started to show results. Divisions began to avoid making products that had no markets and unsold inventory levels declined, contributing to improved turnover of assets.

Then, finally, came the withdrawal from unprofitable lines, starting with the shutting down of the personal computer division in California. This was akin to shock therapy and left a profound impression on company reforms. The orders came in succession to stop making and selling PCs, FLCDs, electric typewriters, optical cards for data storage, and photovoltaic batteries. This of course was antithetical to the principle of organizing the company along divisional lines.

Once the decision was made to drop unprofitable business operations, Mitarai then turned to the second phase of reconstruction. Next would be an even greater challenge: the total reformation of Canon and its corporate culture.

2

Turning Conventional Wisdom on its Head: The Production Reformation

SAYONARA TO THE CONVEYOR BELT

Tadao Yamada, a general manager at Nagahama Canon, a manufacturing subsidiary located about 300 kilometers west of Tokyo, ground his teeth in suppressed anger. It was July 12, 1997, and a group of visitors were issuing a stream of criticisms, saying the traditional conveyor-belt assembly line at the site was out of date.

Normally, Yamada was a calm individual. But he had nurtured the production line at Nagahama Canon from the outset and had overseen the start-up of production in October 1988. To hear visitors deride the factory's sparkling new automated warehouse, with its conveyor-belt assembly line and unmanned transport system, was barely tolerable.

The main line of business at Nagahama Canon was supplying laser printers for Hewlett-Packard and other companies on an original equipment manufacturer (OEM) basis. The plant also produced cartridges for inkjet printers. The Peripheral Products Operations at Canon headquarters handled OEM sales, and consigned orders to Nagahama Canon. Laser printers are office workhorses; the annual worldwide market scale is roughly 12 million units. If its OEM business is included, Canon dominates the world market for laser printers, with a share of over 60%.

Introduction of the cell method

In September 1997, Mitarai paid a visit to the manufacturing arm of a major electronics company, accompanied by Canon directors. The company had ceased assembly-line production and switched to so-called cell production, involving small teams of workers who produced the entire product in multiple steps, with the conveyor belt completely eliminated.

"That experience was eye-opening," said Mitarai. "We need to revolutionize our production this way. How about trying it out at Nagahama?"

Mitarai's suggestion spurred the company to action. By October, the Production Reformation Promotion Committee, set up in Peripheral Products Operations, got under way, designating Nagahama Canon as a model plant. The kickoff ceremony for plant reform was held in December and the movement got under way officially from the start of 1998.

Cell production also entailed risks. Compared with electrical components or home-use TV game units, laser printers are large items and difficult to assemble by cell units. Or at least that's the way Yamada felt. So he started with a campaign called *ma-jime* ("closing the gap").

The objective of *ma-jime* was to reduce or eliminate the unnecessary operations from a conveyor-belt assembly line. This kind of campaign can be easily understood on the factory floor. In addition to reducing the distance between workers on the assembly line, the plant layout was modified to shorten the distance that the components had to be conveyed. This facilitated workers' operations involving parts and improved efficiency. As a result of opening up more space at the factory, it was now possible to locate the packaging operations — which had previously been performed at a separate line — beside the line that assembled laser printers. The merging of assembly and packaging gave a marked boost to efficiency.

With the *ma-jime* improvements under way, the next step was an experiment in which the assembly of laser scanners — a major component of the laser printer — was taken off the conveyor and shifted to cell production. The thinking behind this was that it would be too risky to attempt to switch all assembly work from conveyor to cell, but it would be comparatively simple to entrust cells with the assembly of components smaller than the finished product. The length of the line where the scanner units were assembled was about 20 meters, no more than one-tenth that of the line used for the main units. It seemed right for this kind of experimentation.

Reaction and rebellion on the factory floor

As the production reformation campaign got under way, outside consultants began conducting training sessions to change worker awareness. Sessions began with emphasis on such basics as exchanging greetings properly. Initially, some resistance surfaced. Since at that time results of the *ma-jime* campaign had not become evident, others complained that cell production made the work floor more cramped.

Despite the evident confusion, the company proceeded to make preparations for the full-fledged implementation of the cell-production system for the manufacture of laser printers. According to Yamada's calculations, switching to cells would make it possible to sharply improve production technology. The cells already at work assembling the scanner units were going smoothly, leading management to conclude that they needed to try it across the entire process.

In April 1998, the first trials began. Six lines had been in operation assembling the printer units. Rather than switch over to cells all at once, the change was done one line at a time. The ultimate version of cell production called for one worker assembling each item but Canon opted for cells in which the operation was performed by a team of 10 workers. Great care was taken with the preparations for this.

The cells encountered an unexpected initial setback: productivity did not increase even slightly. Checks of the figures showed that, if anything, productivity was even lower than on the assembly lines. Yamada and other responsible individuals at the production site huddled together. From the standpoint of dissatisfaction on the factory floor alone, this was fast turning into a worst-case scenario.

Then a miracle appeared, in the form of women on the job who took the initiative, forming all-women teams composed of 10 members. Acting entirely on their own, they organized meetings and began to mull over ways to improve operations. While some dissatisfaction lingered, they became increasingly familiar with the cells. The all-women teams were able to realize their production targets three days after they began their meetings.

Previously, factory workers did their tasks in synch with the speed of the conveyor belt. With cells, assembly work proceeded at each worker's individual pace. This is the greatest merit of the cell system and was expected to be an advantage for workers as well. Unfortunately, immediately following the switchover to the cell system, some workers who had grown used to assembly-line work found themselves unable to adapt to more flexible production speeds. But production workers gradually adapted themselves to the new regime and even imposed their own changes on some stages of operation. The benefits of *ma-jime* in enabling the merger of production and packaging processes were clear for all to see. Gradually, the grumbles and friction began to disappear.

Cell system's merits become evident

Workers began producing their own devices to match the cell operations. Previously such devices, which had been designed for conveyor-belt production, had been ordered from specialist suppliers outside the company and boasted specifications higher than necessary. But bulky equipment used by assembly lines were difficult for cells to use. In the more confined area where *ma-jime* work was performed, those on the job began thinking that it would be more sensible for all concerned if they were to make more compact, lighter equipment to facilitate production work themselves. Workers at Nagahama Canon called the handmade devices they created *karakuri* (gizmos). They were designed to function well, most without motors or power.

The purpose-built machines had the added advantage of reducing equipment costs. For example, the image-evaluation test equipment used to check on printing precision was as large as an office copier and cost ¥6 million. A new type, developed inhouse, was reduced to desktop size and cost about ¥500,000. The device used to transport components was trimmed of motors and other bulky parts and was finally reduced to a small handcart. The big automated warehouse was shut down and replaced by a system under which the minimum number of parts was placed at predetermined sites.

These amendments on the production side had an immediate impact on productivity. Workers who had been attached to the production lines made the rounds to other departments, becoming known as *katsu-jin*, loosely translated as "people whose abilities can be made use of elsewhere in the company". This was an interesting way of bringing flexibility to the formal rules of personnel assignments. These workers do not merely make the rounds; they are transferred to work on the production lines of different products or to new departments altogether. Another way to look at it would be that they represent the number of additional production-line workers that would be required now to achieve the same level of productivity had the cell-production method never been introduced. Numbering 212 in 1998, their figure rose to 280 in 1999, and 728 (all numbers cumulative) by 2000. Since the total number of workers at Nagahama Canon, including regular staff, part-timers and workers seconded by subcontractors, had been 2,600 in 1998, the number of these special staff had risen to one-tenth of the entire labor force. By 2001, when the number of workers had fallen below 2,000, their impact increased further. By Nagahama Canon's calculations, the monetary value from the results of this staff went from ¥530 million in 1998 to ¥610 million in 1999 to ¥720 million in 2000. The gains from space savings grew each year in 10,000 square-meter increments. As a result, even while Nagahama Canon's sales revenues declined, from about ¥130 billion in 1988 to ¥102 billion in 2000, its after-tax profits doubled during this period. In addition to the contributions to improved performance made by a reduction in the labor force and space savings, there was a considerable drop in the inventory of work in process. The time needed for these semi-finished products to become fully finished products also improved.

Yamada's production method could not simply be called a cell system. Nagahama Canon preferred to use the term "prism cell". It was a system developed through a great deal of effort. By June 1999, conveyor-belt assembly lines at Nagahama Canon had ceased to exist. The following August, the huge automated warehouse was also gone.

Reaction of suppliers

The manufacturing reformation at Nagahama Canon continued after the conveyor belts ground to a halt. First came a campaign to get the suppliers involved. Part of the space vacated as a result of the switchover to cell production was leased to vendors who supplied Canon. By allowing them to set up shop inside the factory, Nagahama Canon was able to hold down its parts inventory to minimum levels. The suppliers were also encouraged to adopt their own cells, which enabled them to set up a production system that could respond speedily to the need for greater or less output. Nagahama Canon sent a special team to encourage components suppliers to start their own cell production.

The arrival times of delivery trucks at the Nagahama Canon plant were also adjusted in line with requests from the factory floor, resulting in a virtual elimination of congestion and huge reductions in the time it took to load and unload cargoes.

"In terms of personnel evaluation, we found that the new system allowed us to put stronger emphasis on job perform-ance," says Mitsuo Sawada, general manager of corporate planning at Nagahama Canon. Because working by the cell system involved workers completing tasks individually, it became easier to evaluate each worker's performance. To individuals or groups who greatly exceeded their targets, Nagahama Canon's president, Masaru Muto, would present rewards.

In line with the move to a performance-evaluation system, greater effort went into education and training. A prism cell training center was established at Nagahama Canon and training was conducted before the switchover to cells. The company also prepared its own trainers.

Breaking down the barriers

At the beginning of 2001, Muto began to reconsider the rela-tionship between indirect and direct departments. Direct refers to those at the production site; indirect would include office staff — accounting, finance and administration — as well as production planning and other departments related to production control. Muto turned his attention to produc-tion control, eliminating a specialized section for this and transferring all its functions — from production planning to quality control and inspections — to the factory floor. The production workers themselves took part in planning and quality control.

"Up to that point, the production management depart-ments would receive engineering drawings and drop them off at the production site," says Muto. "Then time was needed to work up production plans."

Nobody, of course, knew the situation on the factory floor better than those who were working there. Having them involved in decisions led to a speeding up of production planning. On the notice boards at the site where finished goods streamed out, the plan and figures showing actual progress would be written in by a worker, so anyone could know the status of operation in the entire factory merely by glancing at the boards.

About 15% of the workers in direct departments, about 70 altogether, were transferred to other sections. After about six months, they returned to their previous jobs and someone else was sent to replace them. The ultimate objective was for all the workers in direct departments to learn the work that was being performed elsewhere at the factory. This would not only make it possible for the staff to respond quickly to rush orders for boosted production but was also done with the aim of removing the distinction between indirect and direct activities.

Muto's ultimate objective was to make Nagahama Canon a factory able to stand up to any and all changes. The greatest merit of the cell system was its flexibility as a production system when compared with the assembly-line method.

An assembly line based on a conveyor system was at its most efficient when producing at full output. But, no matter how much it produced, unless its products were sold, they would only pile up in the warehouse. Cell manufacturing, by contrast, is capable of changing its operating speed to change output. This characteristic is also useful for keeping up good relations with customers.

To give an example, plans for orders used to be submitted three months before delivery but, after adoption of the cell system, this was reduced to two months. Two weeks' advance notification was enough to change the models being produced. Moreover, production flexibility was achieved by the switch to cell-production and this strengthened Canon's position as, in this specific instance, an OEM supplier. For example, Canon could make recommendations that benefited the customer and could more easily adapt to requests for changes. The plant was gradually becoming the kind of place that could stand up to the changes that Muto had envisaged. The prism cell system into which Canon had poured its efforts now extends throughout the Canon group.

THE MEN BEHIND THE REFORMS

Behind the story of how the manufacturing reformation at Nagahama Canon proceeded from its start on the factory floor is yet another story, about the men who instigated the changes: Mitarai and Junji Ichikawa, then deputy group executive of Peripheral Products Operations and now a managing director and group executive in charge of Global Manufacturing Headquarters.

Ichikawa had joined Canon in mid-career, having previously worked for Shiba Denki, a mid-sized electronics manufacturer affiliated with Hitachi. Banking on his successful background in the development of laser printers, he was made the key person in Peripheral Products, entrusted with the OEM business, around 1991.

In the OEM business, producers are under relentless pressure from the buyers to reduce prices. In the case of laser printers, which were enjoying good market growth, the number of units being bought was growing but there was still intense pressure on prices. But, aside from increased production, Canon had no success in reducing its prices; that is, the increase in production was not showing up as a reduced cost — as would normally be expected. Ichikawa decided to investigate the component-procurement method and was surprised to learn that the purchasing costs remained fixed irrespective of the size of the order.

His first step was to set up a "key parts" committee and change the system that delegated authority for procurement to the development side. This enabled procurement costs to be varied according to changes in design or volume of output, thus succeeding in cutting overall procurement costs.

Harnessing this momentum, Ichikawa went looking for other ways to pare costs, making the rounds of other factories in the Canon group and suppliers. This turned out to be the vanguard of the manufacturing reformation.

One of Canon's suppliers was a medium-size manufacturer of floppy disks. This was an extremely cost-competitive market from which Canon had withdrawn, but this particular manufacturer chose to remain in the fray. When Ichikawa asked its sales representative the reason why, the man replied, "Because we make them by hand". Hearing this, Ichikawa experienced an epiphany. Shiba Denki, where he had previously worked, was not that big a company, so developers worked at the factory and were involved in the production technology as well. Armed with these experiences, and also cognizant of production technology trends, he had some degree of familiarity with the idea of the cell system that had begun to infiltrate the electronics industry. Unlike conveyor-belt assembly lines, in cells, the components are passed directly from one worker to another. The phrase "by hand" was the tip-off.

Ichikawa quickly requested the supplier to give him a tour of the factory. Ichikawa was highly impressed by what he had seen; but when he talked things over with the Canon staff assigned to oversee production, he was unable to get his point across.

Looking for a way to clear the logjam, in May 1997 Ichikawa issued a proclamation to his OEM clients that he intended to achieve a manufacturing reformation — this just two months after he had gone to observe cell production at the supplier's. Then in July, the day of reckoning arrived: factory staff from Canon's suppliers came to tour the Nagahama facility.

Getting the president involved

This led to the situation outlined earlier where Tadao Yamada, the general manager in charge of production, and others at Nagahama Canon received a tongue-lashing. Ichikawa had prompted the visitors beforehand to be as tough as possible. So their behavior was actually instigated by Ichikawa. The reaction by the Nagahama Canon people went exactly as hoped. Ichikawa, deciding the time was ripe, approached president Mitarai together with Takashi Kitamura, head of Peripheral Products Operations.

"The cell system offers the best approach to carry out manufacturing reformation," Kitamura told Mitarai. Mitarai had been thinking along the same lines. "We can achieve lower costs right away by farming out orders but that doesn't accomplish more than helping the suppliers push through their own improvements," he said. But Mitarai knew there would be no real reformation until Canon succeeded in boosting its own productivity. Since returning to Japan in 1989, he had been making the rounds to factories each year. He felt, with a growing sense of crisis, that the factories in Japan faced a grim situation as more production went overseas. Something had to be done to keep production in Japan. Then Kitamura and Ichikawa made their pitch and Mitarai leaped at the opportunity. "If there's a company that is succeeding with the cell system, take me to it," Mitarai said. He wouldn't be satisfied without seeing it for himself.

Ichikawa began thinking about where to take his boss. They picked the subsidiary of a major electronics company. In September 1997, just before their inspection tour, Mitarai sat for an orientation and was soon firing a series of questions at his hosts. "I caught on to what they were saying right away," says Mitarai. His group included Ichikawa and Hisashi Sakamaki, then group executive of the Production Management Headquarters (now called Global Manufacturing Headquarters). Sakamaki is now president of Canon Electronics. Also present were Kunio Watanabe, Corporate Planning Development Headquarters' group executive and Muto, the president of Nagahama Canon.

"To have attempted to implement reformation of manufacturing abruptly through the company would have created too much opposition, with greater risk of failure in the end." With this foremost in mind, Mitarai decided to start things off from the Peripherals Division, where the idea for change had initially been proposed. The "New CPS" (New Canon Production System) campaign that had long been in force at Canon's Production Headquarters was still in effect, and could be credited with genuine results. From the viewpoint of Production Headquarters, calls for a quick changeover to the cell system could not be acted upon that easily.

Mitarai, sensing that this indicated resistance on the part of the Production Headquarters, made the decision not to implement the first changes at a factory operated by the parent company but, by having Nagahama Canon go ahead as point man, his strategy was to initiate change on the periphery, and then let it spread towards the heart.

That he was already thinking along these lines before the factory visit is pretty clear from the fact that he included Muto in his entourage. Neither Mitarai nor Ichikawa have raised this point but the two might have worked it out between themselves.

The production reformation initially worked out between Mitarai and Ichikawa could not have been set in motion merely at the whim of top executives. There were also others at work behind the scenes, making adjustments to Ichikawa's ideas between headquarters and the factory. One of these was Masafumi Okukubo, who at the time managed the Peripherals Manufacturing Strategic Planning Department. For about a year after the start of the reformation campaign, Okukubo became something of a permanent fixture at Nagahama Canon. Initially, Okukubo found himself as a buffer between Yamada and the others who felt that cell production might be dangerous, and those who were lined up behind Ichikawa and who wanted it adopted as quickly as possible. Coordinating between the rival camps was a tough assignment. Plant workers looked on those from the headquarters as a sort of occupying army. "Sometimes I feared for my life," says Okukubo, half in jest. Despite these conflicts, Okukubo managed to get the two sides to agree.

MATRIX MANAGEMENT PUSHES REFORMS

After confirming the success of the production reforms at Nagahama Canon, Mitarai's next endeavor was to transplant cell production to other factories.

One tool that paved the way for the expansion of cell production was the launch of a Management Reform Committee in April 1998. The aim of this committee was to cut through the red tape in the various divisions of the company.

The committee, in addition to its own activities, had eight subcommittees dedicated to production and distribution systems (under the Production Reform Committee), development systems (under the Development System Reform Committee), and so on. At Canon, this method to join the compartmentalized organizations became known as "matrix management".

Mitarai carefully picked each member of the subcommittees. For example, he chose Takashi Saito, who at the time served as a chief executive responsible for inkjet printer operations and is now a Canon managing director and deputy managing director of Canon Europe, to chair the Development Reform Subcommittee. Yusuke Emura, a director and chief executive of Office Imaging Products Operations, and as such responsible for the company's copying machine business, was assigned as the second chairman of the Production Reform Subcommittee. Emura is now a managing director and group executive of the Global Environment Promotion Headquarters.

The attempts at reform encountered constant open and hidden forms of resistance from the bureaucracy — a phenomenon by no means unique to Canon. Mitarai was concerned that if the special committees were made up only of specialized staff, this would invite more resistance. So, instead, he assigned top management to the committees to minimize resistance. If the head of one of the committees proposed a project that would affect the entire company — the adoption of cell manufacturing, for instance — then the other top managers would be obliged to go along. Why? Because they would want his endorsement of other projects that they might propose. It would be reciprocal.

Chipping away at resistance

Working through the Management Reform Committee, Canon was able to achieve the results Mitarai sought. That committee ceased to function at the end of 2000 and was reincarnated the following year as the Management Strategy Committee. The first plant to be targeted for adoption of cell-style production was the one at Toride, in Ibaraki Prefecture, northeast of Tokyo, which at the time served as the company's main facility for production of copiers, laser printers and other office equipment. Those on the factory side were convinced the cell system would be difficult to adopt for copiers, because their construction was considerably more complex than that of laser printers.

So Mitarai got around the problem by splitting the factory into two, and adopting the cell system for the printers, believing that the system that had worked successfully at Nagahama Canon would go smoothly at Toride as well.

After watching the cell system succeed for laser printers at Toride, the copier section of the plant also decided to make the switch. It had previously run nine 120-meter-long assembly lines, but by 1999 all of these were gone. The number of high-speed digital-copier units produced per worker using the cell system was fewer than for conveyor-belt assembly, but once the new system took root, the cells more than doubled output. At the same time, workers made their own assembly tools. One example of this was the development of a handmade ramp for the wheeled tables used for moving the copiers being assembled, replacing the cranes that had been used previously. Costing ¥30,000 to produce, these ramps resulted in considerable savings in equipment costs. The same kind of building of special equipment that had occurred at Nagahama began to occur at Toride.

When Mitarai showed up at Toride, he was moved by how workers had put their knowledge to work and developed simple and inexpensive implements. This led him to coin the word *chie*-tech, "knowledge-based technology", and from then on this new word was applied whenever Canon factories developed tools and equipment on site.

"Don't let this be a one-time event," said Mitarai. "Let's spread this approach through the whole company." These were the first words Mitarai said to Yusuke Emura in April 1999, when the latter became chief executive of the Production Center, having previously headed the Image Office Equipment Division. He had been somewhat disdainful at what he had seen taking place at Nagahama Canon, but now he changed his mind and supported it.

In August 1999, Mitarai convened a gathering of members of the Management Reform Committee at Nagahama Canon, which had by that time completely eliminated conveyor-belt assembly. The 12 participants, mainly company directors, were brought together to show off the results of the production reformation at Nagahama Canon to convince them the method could work elsewhere in the company.

During 1999, the cell system was put into operation at the Oita Canon camera plant in Kyushu; the Canon Chemicals plant in Ibaraki; and Canon's main inkjet printer plant in Fukushima, amongst others. In July, when Emura initiated cell production in Oita, he said, "This should set off the process through the whole company." This was the year that selected staff from factories around Japan converged on Nagahama Canon and set up a Cell Production Study Group to identify and work out potential problems.

As part of the process by which the cell system was propagated, trainers who would serve to instruct at production sites also began their studies. Initially, outside consultants were used but, before long, Canon workers themselves were teaching, and adding their own repertoire. By 2001, a total of 3,000 people had been coached so that they could provide training.

Canon cell production at the Ami Plant, near Tokyo

Overseas, the cell system got under way from 2000, beginning with a kickoff ceremony attended by the presidents of 10 of Canon's overseas factories. People at the overseas factories also knew about the changes being wrought in Japan. Some of them had already begun to imitate certain parts of the process. But because of differences in language and culture, the shift overseas was difficult. Emura assigned 20 trainers who were of plant-manager class to make the rounds overseas, together with 50 assistants. "Let them see what you do, and if you can make the local workers see the results, they'll take your word for it," he said.

Canon's manufacturing reforms were initiated from the top down. While those on the factory floor could be counted on to continue to come up with suggestions for cutting waste, sweeping changes, such as the switchover to cell production, were unlikely to occur from the bottom up. When Mitarai took his first look at the cell system, the revelation he experienced was more than simply seeing it as an improvement; it paved the way towards an optimized situation for all concerned.

ELIMINATING EXCESS

To Mitarai, cell production's greatest appeal was its flexibility in enabling changes in the volume of output. With their mature markets, advanced economies could no longer hope for expansive growth; what's more, Japan was suffering from severe deflation. In such times, the ability to boost production immediately to meet demand, and reduce or halt it when demand falls, is of paramount concern. This requires astute and flexible manufacturing of a variety of goods in small lots. Mass production with limited product variation, as is performed on conveyor-belt assembly lines, not only results in lost sales opportunities but runs greater risks of stockpiling larger inventories. Considering the huge investment outlays needed for production equipment, mass production of one or a few items places a heavier burden on any company's management in procuring added investment for financing as well as expenses for storage and related costs. The slump in electronics and telecommunications industries resulting from the bursting of the tech bubble in 2001 triggered excess production, which also resulted in burgeoning inventories.

Many of Japan's corporate executives do not fully understand the real threat posed by excess investment and production. Those whose sole business experience was marked by success during the period of high growth and expanding markets may delude themselves into thinking that even if they over-invest, they'll recover it somewhere down the road. Or that they can manage excess inventories but can't risk lost opportunities.

Cell production is understood by any specialist in production management but has not, until very recently, been widely used. One reason for this is quite simple: the conveyor assembly system has been largely successful up to now. Production of goods for which steady growth is assured is ideal for conveyor-belt assembly. For that matter, companies like Canon, which are used to expansion and growth, tended to see massive conveyor-belt production systems as symbols of growth and progress.

Another constraint is a lingering belief in the merits of standardization and division of labor, by which things would be standardized so that anyone could perform the tasks, as a means of raising production efficiency. This was the "Fordism" espoused by American auto magnate Henry Ford. Although Toyota Motor Co. was in the process of shattering this long-held myth, it still had its believers. Perhaps because the Toyota system was seen as being intertwined with the company's distinct corporate culture, and thus difficult to comprehend from the outsider's view, many people attributed the improvements it carried out to Fordism. There was also the belief, still in effect when cell production began at Canon, that cells could not be used to produce large items. True, cells could not be applied to products as big as automobiles, but Canon proved it would work for copiers.

How cash-flow management changed the workplace

That Mitarai was not fazed by this apparent bias was due to his instinctive grasp of cash-flow management. If cash flow is strongly emphasized, then any items that become fixed assets — such as large equipment and inventories or support systems — are all regarded as undesirable. Likewise for anything that slows the production process, such as model changes. The worst thing of all, however, is creating sales revenues through channel stuffing; namely, forcing finished-product inventory caused by excess production onto sales companies.

In fact, with the introduction of the cell system, Canon's cash flow underwent dramatic improvement. For the accounting year ending in December 1997, the free cash flow was −¥23 billion on a consolidated basis. By December 1998, this had been turned around, to a surplus of ¥31 billion; in 1999, this figure had further increased to ¥108 billion; and by December 2000, free cash flow had swollen to ¥134 billion. Support systems and parts inventories — which were ¥100 billion at the end of 1998 — had dropped to ¥85 billion by the end of 1999.

Furthermore, the improvements had the benefit of reducing requirements to the extent of 9,900 workers and the equivalent of 380,000 square meters of space. This was the total floor area and number of plant workers needed at production facilities of the Canon group worldwide during the two years from 1998 to 2000. With 380,000 square meters of space, Canon could construct five to six large factories. The total length of conveyor-belt assembly lines phased out during this period exceeded 16 kilometers. The floor area of automated warehouses eliminated reached 16,800 square meters. Another 80,000 square meters of leased warehouse facilities became unnecessary, saving about ¥1 billion in annual costs. The freeing up of workers and space, by Canon's own account, had the net effect of saving ¥11.7 billion in 2000. The production reforms centered on cell production thus did far more than simply rationalize factory operations; they generated cash from within the company's own assets.

Linking the top with the workplace

Canon was by no means the only company to introduce cell manufacturing; other examples can be found among major electronics firms and component-makers. What makes Canon exceptional is that from the start of the reforms at Nagahama Canon, the system had spread to virtually all its factories within just two years. For this to take place over such a brief period, and to spread through the entire group, is rare in Japan. While many Japanese firms have adopted the system piecemeal, no other company can show such clear results as the improvement in cash flow. And this can be credited largely to the efforts of Mitarai himself.

Having said that, it's unlikely that the manufacturing reformation would have succeeded solely on the efforts of men at the top such as Mitarai and Ichikawa. Remember the women working on the factory floor, who worked out ways to over-come the initial awkwardness when the cell system was begun? Without the energy percolating from the bottom up, includ-ing innovations and a variety of techniques, it couldn't have happened. It was not the cell formula per se — as the people at Nagahama Canon stress repeatedly. Without the expertise of those on the factory floor, the cells wouldn't have worked.

Fordism's standardized mass-production lines, with their division of labor, tended to downplay individual skills. The level accepted as standard was set as the average worker's ability or slightly below that. The efforts of employees on the factory floor did not enter the equation. The cell system, by contrast, brings out each individual's latent skills. This is also in accord with Canon's tradition of placing importance on worker independence.

One more thing that shouldn't be overlooked is the pres-ence of Okukubo, manager of planning in the Peripheral Products Operations. In the initial stages of the reform process, when there was a gap between the thinking of those at the top and those on the factory floor, he served as a lubricant between the two sides. If the thoughts of those on opposite ends had not been reconciled, it's unlikely the reformation would have succeeded. When use of the cell system spread from Nagahama Canon to other factories, he leaped into the fray, serving as a fixer. Others were involved in similar roles. One such person was Katsuyuki Hiraishi, who oversaw the adoption of cell production for laser printers at the Toride Plant. (Hiraishi is now deputy group executive of the Global Manufacturing Headquarters.) As a "missionary" who joined Okukubo in promulgating the cell system, he made the rounds through Japan, and traveled overseas to China and other Asian countries. Muto was another who played a leading role as a fixer.

With ideas from the top and enthusiasm from the bottom, the success was clearly more than a top-down development. Nor did it happen from the bottom up. Rather, it was, reverberations from both that provided Canon's manufacturing reformation with the necessary drive. The dynamic interplay between the two is symbolic of Canon's ongoing reformation.

THE CHALLENGE OF CHINA

The strongest motive for reforming production was the accelerating pace at which production was moving abroad. The sense of crisis was particularly acute toward China, with its advantage of low labor costs. The changeover to cell production gave the company a system that was particularly receptive to change. It also boosted cost competitiveness. But the Chinese threat did not subside. Even at Nagahama Canon, with its bolstered earnings structure, the workforce and sales both declined. The operations continued to shrink.

Moving to China

Within the Canon group, the pace picked up for the transfer of production to China. Rival makers, including Ricoh and Fuji Xerox, had already set up copier operations in the country. Copiers are more complex than many other products and assembly is comparatively difficult. Perhaps because of Mitarai's influence, Canon wanted to keep its production in Japan. Previously, its copiers that were aimed at small business had been produced in China and Canon had begun preparations to transfer nearly all of its copier models from mid-range and below. Together with Canon Aptex (this company was merged with Copyer on January 1, 2003 to form Canon Finetech) and another subsidiary, the company built China's largest copier plant at Suzhou, Jiangsu Province. It started production in July 2002. The total investment on the plant's first stage was more than ¥10 billion. In addition to serving as a base for worldwide exports, the plant also obtained permission to sell in the domestic market.

In September 2001, Canon established a fully-owned Chinese subsidiary and obtained 230,000 square meters of land. A 71,000-square meter plant was built in the first stage. Aptex and Copyer also set up a fully owned local subsidiary that would lease the factory. Plans were for Canon to produce a medium-priced copier with a speed of 30 pages per minute, and a popularly priced model with a speed of less than 20 pages per minute, while Aptex would make paper feeders and other components. By 2004, the plant plans to employ some 3,500 workers and produce 20,000 units per month, with sales valued at ¥200 billion.

Ultimately, a full one-third of the copiers sold by the Canon group are to be produced in China. The operation of the plant in China would coincide with the transfer of production of mid-range and popularly priced copiers from the Toride Plant.

Chinese production of the same laser printers that were being made at Canon Nagahama was expanding. Up to that point, some were being made at a subsidiary's plant in Zhuhai, Guangdong Province, but since it had no surplus capacity, a second facility was set up in Dalian, Liaoning Province.

The Dalian subsidiary had up to that point been producing toner cartridges and containers for laser printers. An additional ¥2 billion was invested and about 200 more workers were hired. Such basic components as the discharge lamp and optical components were shipped from Japan. The main line was a mid-range model priced to sell at ¥150,000 in the Japanese market. Within two years, the plant was expected to boost production from 40,000 units a month to twice that figure.

Canon Zhuhai, in Guangdong Province, one of Canon's largest production facilities in China

Production of laser printers began at Zhongshan, Guangdong Province, in 2001. The manufacturing subsidiary was funded entirely by Canon. Production of scanners for home use, which had been divided between Taiwan and mainland China, were now to be concentrated in China. After first phasing out Taiwan's production of general-use models, next-generation models would be produced at factories in China. Afterwards, the percentage of production in China would gradually increase. During 2000, production at the Zhuhai manufacturing subsidiary — mainly of upscale models — reached half of total output. The remainder of output was split evenly between locally owned factories in Taiwan and non-affiliated companies elsewhere on the mainland.

Copiers, laser printers and scanners are all products with a promise of growth. In 2000, the total number of copiers shipped to Japanese companies, including those abroad, reached 1.7 million units, a year-on-year decline of 3%. But as companies are in the process of replacing their older units with digital models, the mid- to long-term prospects were for further growth of the market.

Laser printers for offices were moving well, and Canon anticipated the world market to grow at about 10% annually in the future. The market for scanners is beset by plunging prices resulting from heated competition.

Low-cost China

The major reason for concentrating production in China was low labor costs. The average annual wage in China in 1999 stood at about US$1,000, or about 3% of what the same worker would earn in Japan. With a population that far surpasses that of Southeast Asia, there is a strong likelihood that China's wage levels will remain low for the foreseeable future.

The workers are quick to learn their tasks and at the Zhuhai plant, which produces scanners, rows of female workers can be seen mounting tiny components the size of grains of rice onto circuit boards at lightning speed, the entire process done by hand. An automatic mounter built in Japan would operate more efficiently than their manual work but, considering the added time needed to retool the machine to produce boards for other products, manual mounting is faster.

Another of China's strengths is the hidden growth potential of an enormous market. Take copiers, for example, where the market is growing at over 10% a year. In 2000, Fuji Xerox obtained rights from Xerox to sell copiers produced at their jointly operated factory in China. Ricoh also entered the Chinese market in 1997 through a joint venture with a Chinese company, and has been producing copiers.

Muto of Nagahama Canon, Hiraishi and others made frequent visits to production sites in China, where they passed on many aspects of the *chie*-tech they had spun out. Since it was all in the family, so to speak, there was no way around it, but Muto admits he had mixed feelings. The knowledge he and the others passed on boosted productivity at the Chinese factories; as a consequence, the competitiveness of Nagahama

Canon and other factories in Japan declined in relative terms. Production of digital full-color copiers and other high added-value products was transferred from the mass-production divisions of the Toride Plant to the nearby plant at Ami in Ibaraki Prefecture, with production of the remaining products shifting to China, Thailand or other overseas factories. The Toride Plant itself became the center for production planning tests, technical instruction and other operations prior to the large-scale production of new products at other domestic or foreign factories.

SUPPLY-CHAIN MANAGEMENT (SCM) — CANON-STYLE

Holding the line against China's lower costs could not be done by reforming the factories alone. For the company to survive, it was likely that the entire business process — R&D, design, basic materials and components procurement, distribution, sales, marketing and so on — would have to be interactively linked. This meant not merely coming up with the best possible arrangement at each level, but working out the best possible arrangement for the entire business process. "If improvements at the factory level alone were counted in terms of one point, improvements that would combine all the divisions together would be 300 points," said Hiraishi. Even at Nagahama Canon, reforms in procurement had led to a thorough review of relations with suppliers, and moves were under way to extend this through the entire Canon organization.

This technique of linking all the parts of a company is referred to as supply-chain management, or SCM. With SCM, it is possible to link the flow of work between the divisions and control the entire operation. Its singular characteristic is how production is increased or decreased dynamically in response to sales channels and inventory. Similar concepts had been around in the past but were limited by the power of the available technology to do so. With today's more powerful technology and software, all parts of a company can be linked in a streamlined workflow.

In October 2001, Canon's copier division put into operation an SCM system in the U.S. and Japan that enabled confirmation of copier inventories. At the start of each month, the copier division holds a Production and Sales Meeting. Previously during such meetings, the factories handling production would first receive an accurate report covering sales and inventory and then, based on this, would produce a monthly sales plan for production that would commence two months later. Following the adoption of SCM, however, the factory staff can investigate inventories on a daily basis and revise the production plan on a weekly basis. This reduces the lead time — from the receipt of a sales order to shipment from the factory — from three months to one month. With production plans fine-tuned on a weekly basis, production start-ups can be expedited, and the results are spectacular. When SCM was introduced experimentally for a mid-range copier model, inventory levels fell from two months to less than one month. When extended to the entire product line, SCM promises considerable cost savings.

Preparing to go global

One barrier that stood in the way of expanding SCM to the entire product range was disparities in the product codes. Each Canon product carries a label bearing a bar code, referred to as the product code, that made it possible — in theory at least — to monitor the number of units shipped from the factory or warehouse. But there was no uniformity to this system: the codes were completely different at each sales company and manufacturing subsidiary around the world.

Canon deals with 157 sales companies around the world, handling as many as 200,000 product codes. With affiliates adding new codes and modifying existing ones, it was difficult for management to synchronize the entire process. As the Canon group became increasingly diversified and internationalized, its affiliates around the world organized their own unique systems and, with them, their own product codes. This was because each overseas affiliate put a higher priority on its own needs than on linking its systems with Canon headquarters. As long as the product codes were not standardized, it was almost impossible to obtain an overall view of inventories within the group as a whole.

In April 1999, a subcommittee headed by senior managing director Yukio Yamashita, under the umbrella of the Management Reform Committee, embarked on a project to standardize product codes on a global basis. With Mitarai's blessing, the project was given high priority. Opposition from local operations, however, proved unexpectedly high. Since the top priority of the Canon subsidiaries was to expand their own businesses, they were reluctant to get involved in a project which carried no promise of profit. Not wanting to be saddled with an extra burden to accommodate the wishes of the parent company, they preferred to give priority to systems more closely linked to their local situation.

"Without the president's strong support, we never could have pulled it off," says Toshiaki Asano, now senior general manager of the Creative Engineering Environment Development Center and the man who was actually entrusted with the task of standardizing the product codes. When meeting executives of the overseas subsidiaries, Mitarai explained the necessity of standardized product codes. A top-level decision called for the standardization process to be completed by July 2001. Once this had been achieved, a system to be called "Mercury" would get under way from September. It anticipated that the job of standardizing all the codes would take over two years to accomplish. Using Mercury, the standardized codes would be assigned from the Japan headquarters to subsidiaries and affiliates around the world. The existing inventories were fitted with new product code labels. Thanks to the Mercury system, the copier division was also able to start its SCM program. Prior to the introduction of SCM, it was a messy effort to standardize product codes.

Controlling inventory levels

Once SCM takes root, the roles of the factories, division head-quarters and sales companies undergo dramatic changes. At present, the division headquarters has the authority to produce the monthly production plan. In principle, this authority is transferred to the factory, and the main tasks of the head office become the development of new products, planning sales promotion campaigns, and so on. Sales companies in Japan and overseas are relieved of the authority to determine their own inventories. Even the domestic marketing arm, Canon Sales, a public company, is no exception.

The volume of inventory that the entire group should maintain is traditionally determined from the start of the manufacturing process. With SCM in operation, inventory levels can be changed as needed.

The cell-production system has proved to be highly compatible with SCM. Multiple cells, which produce a variety of models, are well suited for this kind of varied-product, small-volume production. SCM, which aims at increasing or decreasing output matched to changes in demand, is difficult to adapt to conveyor-belt assembly-line production. Thus the switchover to cell production was all the more reason why SCM could be established. In a sense, it could even be said that SCM is actually just an extended form of cell production. While cell production has had a major impact on Canon's improved cash flow as a result of reduced inventory and other factors, its expansion to SCM brings with it the promise of even greater results through a more focused use of capital.

Smoothing the edges: Net procurement

In January 2001, 11 Canon companies involved in domestic Japanese operations commenced the full-scale introduction of "net procurement", by which components and materials would be procured via the Internet from some 1,300 suppliers. This would mean that 95% of the annual purchases of upwards of ¥1 trillion in materials would be conducted via the Internet.

"Please continue to visit Canon for sales calls," said Junkichi Kaneko, executive director of Canon's Procurement Center, at orientation meetings conducted for executives of parts-supplier companies at five locations around Japan. Even after moving to the Net, he vowed, face-to-face sales meetings would continue.

Net procurement involves the use of email for everything from estimates, orders and settlement to the furnishing of design diagrams. Using the Internet also has the advantage of lowering costs for component manufacturers, allowing them to focus their efforts on technological development and other work. Net procurement is working to reinforce Canon's overall strengths, including ties with its suppliers.

For SCM to move smoothly, it is essential to raise the ratio of electronic procurement because of the need to greatly reduce lead time and position component orders as close as possible to the date production commences. One example of how this has been achieved can be seen in the copier division, where the delivery of parts was reduced from five-to-10 days prior to production to two-to-four days.

Canon wants to be able to advise component manufacturers of its production plans at an early stage and to receive a speedy response. For small- and medium-size suppliers that do not utilize value-added networks (VANs) or dedicated circuits, accurate and speedy notification of production plans can be made via the Internet. Leased circuit charges and specialized terminals run up VAN costs, and place a heavy burden on small-volume suppliers. The Internet is ideal for these smaller transactions, and electronic procurements that have until now been conducted via LANs or dedicated circuits are, increasingly, shifting to the Internet.

TAKING REFORMS TO THE SALES COMPANIES

Canon Sales, Canon's domestic sales arm, began moves to incorporate SCM into its reforms. The first step was adoption of Sales Force Automation (SFA) by the regional sales companies that handled copiers under the Canon Sales umbrella. SFA is set up to manage progress of the status of activities and sales negotiations by sales staff, and is expected to prove useful in raising sales efficiency.

Canon B.M. Tokyo handles sales of copiers and other office equipment in the metropolitan area. In October 2000, the company adopted SFA. Now, when the company's 186 sales-people return from their sales calls, they go straight to their computer terminal and enter a record of the call, inputting such data as the customer's name, type of business, progress in negotiations, the salesperson's remarks, and so on. The sales supervisor can review these and provide encouragement or advice in a manner that allows him to check activities at separate sales offices on a daily basis.

The sales log can be reviewed not only by managers but by each salesperson's colleagues as well. Entering successes and failures into a database format shared by the entire staff is conducive to improving sales activities. "Rather than depending on the acumen or effort of individual sales staff, we are aiming to boost the abilities of the entire sales organization," says Mitsuo Yanagi, general manager of the Tokyo Image Data Sales Promotion Division at Canon B.M. Tokyo.

Using SFA, the number of calls on new clients, progress in sales negotiations and so on can be processed statistically, and the number of sales contracts concluded by the entire company can be projected. This in turn becomes a weapon for empowering advancement of SCM through the entire Canon group, in much the same way as net procurement. Just as SCM is used to switch production plans from a monthly to a weekly basis, sales companies both in Japan and abroad can change their sales plans along the same timeframe. The contract projection generated by SFA can be linked to an accurate weekly sales projection.

The nine copier sales companies operating under the umbrella of Canon Sales completed their adoption of SFA by the spring of 2001. When Canon completes implementation of SCM, it will be able to assemble data from sales plans submitted by overseas and domestic sales subsidiaries to determine the inventory status of the entire group. This can then be used for generating idealized production plans, which in turn will enable the factories to apportion the needed manpower based on each phase of production. The day is approaching when the production divisions will be able to harness the full power of a completely optimized system organically linked to procurement, sales and other divisions in the company.

Canon sales shifts to software

In the 2000 business year, Canon Sales, which is listed on the Tokyo Stock Exchange, reported consolidated performance figures of ¥795 billion in sales; ¥187 billion in profit; and ¥64 billion in net profit. The company, which employs 7,300, is the main force behind sales of Canon-brand copiers, printers and other products in Japan. Many times there have been rumors that Canon Sales was on the verge of a merger with its parent company, Canon Inc., a move that Mitarai says is impossible.

"I'd rather see them develop their own distinct business," he says. In other words, the company is free, if it so chooses, to handle goods other than Canon's.

"Our sales target is ¥1 trillion," says Haruo Murase, president of Canon Sales. "Software represents about 20% of our present sales; we'd like to boost this to about half." In other words, the company has set its sights on moving energetically from straight sales of Canon-brand products to software and other types of products designed to work in combination with the hardware, such as a document management system — that is, into the solutions business.

Unfortunately, expansion of the solutions business faces two major stumbling blocks: mismatching of human resources, and insufficient software-development capability. On the one hand, Canon Sales lacks a sufficient number of system engineers, a prerequisite for the solutions business; on the other, it has too many "old-style" sales personnel. Murase put a lot of time into considering how he could reshuffle his staff. Software development is being done at Canon's Kosugi

Office, but Kosugi is not able to respond to every single proposal. This led Canon Sales to begin setting up its own software-development capacity.

While ostensibly free to go its own way, the attitude at Canon Sales is still strongly tied to the parent company. One example of this is the SFA linked to SCM. Canon Sales was pulled along by the powerful leadership of former chairman Seiichi Takigawa, but Murase, a more affable type, had worked with Mitarai in the U.S. and preferred to move in parallel. It became increasingly apparent that the company would stay positioned as a member of the Canon group.

Even if SCM could be fully worked out, the company might not have the strength to resist the temptation of low cost afforded by production in China because of considerable differences between labor and other personnel costs in Japan and China. Notwithstanding, China could also be expected to introduce its own SCM and other innovations. "Labor-intensive industries will continue to move out of Japan. The only way to survive will be through industries that provide high added value," says Mitarai.

WHAT TO LEAVE BEHIND?

So then, what will remain in Japan? Device industries, is Mitarai's answer. An example of such products, he points out, would be businesses such as those used by chemical processing factories, which operate 24/7/365. In Canon's case, these would be accessories for copiers and printers — such items as toner, ink, ink tanks and other products.

"Device industries can get by with an extremely small number of workers looking after them," says Mitarai. "That lets higher efficiency absorb the higher labor costs. And it's easier to deal with the foreign-exchange fluctuations as well. The time will come when we will have to respond to calls to move to device-type manufacturing."

This type of manufacturing calls up the image of industries such as steel and chemicals, but Canon envisages something quite different. "Through improvements of existing devices, we can keep getting closer to single functions. If you're going to manufacture in volume, this is done by increasing the number of machines," says Yusuke Emura, one of the chairmen of Canon's Production Reform Subcommittee. In other words, the objective is to produce items using arrays of small, single-function machines. If a product is to be changed, this can be done by simply altering the way the machines are combined. If demand changes, production can be increased or reduced by adding or reducing the number of machines that make up the system. Setting up production is as simple as adding or removing components, like children's building blocks. In a way, it's not unlike the cell-assembly process. If Canon can pull it off, it will herald the inception of device industries for compact and lightweight equipment that can be used for production of a variety of products.

Toner, ink, ink tanks and other consumables have provided Canon with a lucrative source of revenue. Production of these high added-value chemical products based on proprietary technologies will, in principle, not move to China or other overseas factories but will continue to be made in Japan. As device industries, they are not susceptible to labor-cost increases, raising the likelihood that production will remain in Japan for the foreseeable future. New jobs will not be created but the factories themselves will remain in operation.

SECRETS OF "THE BLACK BOX"

Hopes for SOI

Canon also has a secret weapon in its device industries business; a new type of silicon wafer called the Silicon-On-Insulator (SOI) wafer. Silicon wafers are the basic material used in the production of semiconductor substrates, on which integrated circuitry is packed to produce semiconductor chips. Ordinarily, silicon oxide is overlaid on the wafer substrate as an insulator, on which a layer of pure crystallized silicon is applied. If silicon alone is used, on conventional wafers an electrical

charge will temporarily linger between the semiconductor circuitry and the silicon substrate, interfering with the operating
speed. The SOI wafer is analogous to the filling between slices of
bread in a sandwich, serving as an insulator that makes it more
difficult for electric properties from the substrate to affect the
chip. Chips on SOI wafers boast processing speeds that are about
30% faster than existing products, and because they prevent
minute leakage of current to the silicon substrate, SOI power
consumption is less than half that of conventional varieties.

Three-layered wafers are currently produced using two
basic methods. One is the SIMOX method, which involves
the injection of oxygen ions into the wafer to form an oxide
layer. The other involves the binding together of two wafers
with oxidized surfaces. Canon developed its SOI wafers using
the latter, to which it added an original formula using
a "water jet" system. Canon's main rivals in this field include
Ivis (U.S.), a group involving Soitech (France) and two
Japanese companies, and Shinetsu Semiconductors and
Mitsubishi Material Silicon, among others. All of these
companies are engaged in competition to boost quality by
improving the flatness and thinness of the crystallized silicon. In the future, SOI wafers are expected to find growing
use in networked home appliances or equipment used in the
telecommunications infrastructure, where chips with high-
speed processing will be needed. SOI costs are five or more
times higher than conventional wafers, but by 2005 they
are projected to account for about 5% of all demand for
wafers.

In an effort to perfect the SOI wafer, Canon has tied up
with Toshiba, its partner in flat-screen displays. Toshiba tests
the chips while providing Canon with technical advice.
Toshiba plans to introduce ultra-small MPUs and system LSI
products by 2004.

Yet another of Canon's "black boxes" is the SED, the strategic
thin-screen display. With South Korean and Taiwanese manufacturers entering the market, there is a risk that the industry may soon find itself embroiled in an international price
war. How will anyone manage to realize profits? To prevent

imitation, Canon has sequestered its SED production knowledge under wraps in its proverbial "black box". It is making its own production equipment and taking steps to prevent this expertise from leaking out. Taking a cue from the lessons learned by Japanese companies that developed plasma displays, Canon is doing whatever it can to keep the new technology to itself in the hope that, if things work out, this will prevent the prices of products from suffering a sharp decline.

Still, in a mature economy, it is consumers that determine prices. Products that are burdened with higher costs will not sell. At present, consumers still consider flat-screen displays too pricey, which means that further price declines will be unavoidable. Once a few manufacturers announce sharp price reductions, the rest will have no choice but to follow suit. Even with its technological secrets safely hidden away, there are limits to the defense Canon can mount.

Such measures as the switch to cell production and the secreting of technology in "black boxes" may buy time for Japanese manufacturing, but they won't be the deciding factors. "There's no end to manufacturing reformation; it continues forever," says Emura.

3

How Canon Revitalized Development

CHIPS WITH EVERYTHING

On returning from the United States when Canon pulled out of the personal computer business, Yoichi Kawabata was assigned to Product Development Operations at the company's Kosugi office, in Kawasaki, a city between Tokyo and Yokohama. This division was the forerunner of what is now Platform Technology Development Headquarters, where Canon does its basic technology research. The division was made up of several project teams, including Computer Technology, to which Kawabata was assigned. He was put in charge of the CT Project Team, which had 10 members from Firepower as its Japanese-national staff.

Although the research environment was in order, Kawabata felt unsettled. For six months, he did not know what work he should do. When he finally emerged from his despondency, an idea began stirring in his mind. Conversation with other employees with whom he shared company housing revolved around the production of semiconductors, a process with which he was familiar. However, almost no one spoke of circuit design. From his experience in the United States, Kawabata felt that Canon should specialize in making semiconductors and outsource the manufacture of products. Although everyone around him was oriented in the opposite direction, he thought that he might make best use of his knowledge and experience by working on circuit design.

When Kawabata was working at Firepower, it had been necessary to combine semiconductors to overcome the limitations on the number of elements that could be concentrated on a single chip. Now, however, it was becoming possible to assign to one chip the functions that previously had to be allocated to several semiconductors. Kawabata took notice of this. The creation of a circuit by giving a single chip the functions of several semiconductors — in other words, putting a computer on a chip — was the concept behind a new field that came to be known as System on Chip (SOC). Kawabata's team was assigned to the SOC Project, which was then combined with work on the design of circuits for sensors. This brought together a range of Kosugi engineers who were working on circuit design.

Once the development infrastructure was in place, Kawabata turned his attention to the matter of making a product. As he made the rounds of the company's operating divisions, trying to sell them on his technology, the response was lukewarm; his project team had no track record to recommend it. After going from one division to another, he finally got some sign of interest from the copier division. This was early in 1997. "Let's give it a try," they told him. The development target for the SOC Project was to come up with a controller, named NADA (Network Adaptive Digital Architecture), for digital copiers.

The first move was for the copier division to set up an intra-division task force of personnel from related departments. Canon frequently uses task forces, finding that this cuts down the clash of egos that can occur between departments and no one can say they weren't consulted. Once a task force is set up, the memorandum announcing its existence has to receive a red seal of approval from all the division heads. While this at times can seem like an inhouse relay race, once it has been accomplished, all goes smoothly. Having gone through the necessary protocols and obtained the necessary authorizations, Kawabata began work on NADA.

When two new copiers, the imageRUNNER iR5000 and iR6000, went on sale in July 2000, their key feature was multi-functionality. Apart from handling routine copy jobs, these machines were capable of collecting and distributing documents in a network and accumulating a large amount of document data in a built-in hard drive

Eliminating waste

Canon made the imageRUNNER copiers into a series, from a top-of-the-line machine down to a popularly priced model. NADA was used in every model. Beyond the positive effects in functionality, — namely, faster processing speed and improved reliability — NADA was also able to achieve cost savings because the same architecture could be used for more than one model.

Expectations were that the range of applications to which NADA could be put would be further widened because it had become possible to use it for a variety of purposes by using part of a circuit on a chip as a discrete block, and putting together as many blocks as needed. Development of a new block meant opening up a new avenue of use. Kawabata dreamed of expanding applications from copiers to printers and fax machines.

At Canon, neither technology nor technical staff are wasted. When particular operations have outlived their usefulness and are closed down, the engineers who had worked on them are reallocated. That's Canon's way. As Ichiro Endo, group executive for Technology Management Headquarters and senior managing director says: "We thought through every imaginable possibility for making the best of our human resources."

DEVELOPING NEW SENSORS

In January 1999, Shigeyuki Matsumoto, who had been team leader for development of the FLCD, took up his post as director of the Semiconductor Device Development Center near Yokohama. Katsumi Komiyama, who had worked with him on FLCD, became deputy director of the Display Development Center, and went on to work on the development of SED, while Matsumoto returned to his old haunts in the semiconductor area.

Matsumoto had dealt with development and mass-production aspects of sensors some time earlier, in Canon's semiconductor division. Under Nobuyoshi Tanaka (who later became a managing director in charge of Corporate Intellectual Property & Legal Headquarters), he had worked at improving BASIS (the Base Storaged Image Sensor) and had developed the automatic-focus device for the EOS series of SLR cameras, as well as high-precision products for use in scanners and ophthalmic equipment. Tanaka had developed BASIS, a proprietary sensor, through a cooperative arrangement with Professor Tadahiro Ohmi, of Tohoku University. During the time he was with the FLCD development team, from 1994 to the end of 1998, however, Matsumoto had had nothing to do with sensors.

In his new role as head of sensor development, Matsumoto announced, "We're going to drop every superfluous project." Development was going to be a matter of deliberate choice, and be concentrated. The focal point was to be a high-performance area sensor that used Complementary Metal-Oxide Semiconductors (CMOS). An area sensor scans the entire surface of a rectangular or square area. The end objective was to develop uses such as the "eye" of digital cameras. Shunsuke Inoue, who had been struggling with a liquid-crystal projector project, was made project leader. Having each tasted defeat, Matsumoto and Inoue were doubly determined that their project would succeed.

The CMOS area sensor made use of part of the structure employed in BASIS. BASIS used the bipolar type of structural element, but this had a more complex structure than the Charge Coupled Devices (CCD) that Sony and others were developing, and even if a line sensor that had its elements arrayed in a row could be made, it was difficult to come up with a structure for two-dimensional areas. For the autofocus function of cameras, this was dealt with by deploying a multiple number of BASIS line sensors. In the case of scanners, a line sensor could take readings for image data while moving. Nevertheless, when it came to using it as the eye of a digital camera, the sensor just couldn't work with the area to be covered. When the sensor was exposed to light, it had to process data for the same area and shape as the film to be exposed. CMOS had a much simpler structure than BASIS, because the emitter and a number of other functions had been stripped from it. Now it became possible to line up elements to make an area.

Companies other than Canon were working on the development of a CMOS area sensor at that time, and at least some of them were marketing a product. Although the CMOS area sensors used less energy and were cheaper than CCDs, they had a reputation for having poor image quality.

Matsumoto's expectation was that it had to have good image quality, and that had been the philosophy underlying the project to develop a device for eliminating noise — and for which a patent had been granted — that he had developed while working on BASIS. If a bipolar element is taken to be an automobile, it would be a Ferrari — plenty of speed but not easy to operate. BASIS too was like that. It was sensitive enough but Matsumoto and his team had been troubled by what is called "shot noise," noise that lasts a fraction of a second. One of the methods they developed to eliminate noise was to create one circuit for output of both the optical signal that has been detected and the noise, and another circuit for output of the noise only, and to take the second away from the first. The principle was simple but the trick was to ensure that the structure would not become complex once they were added to the elements.

Applying this technology to the CMOS area sensor, Matsumoto succeeded in developing a 3.45-million-pixel sensor that could read a high-quality image at a high speed. This was used in the high-grade EOS D30 digital SLR camera that Canon started selling in October of 2000. According to Canon, the energy consumption is a fifth of that used by a CCD of the same class, which made it possible to reduce the camera's overall energy consumption by about 20%. "If you pick up this camera and a camera of the same class made by some other company, you can't help noticing a difference in weight. Because we cut energy consumption, the battery is much smaller; that's what makes it lighter," Matsumoto says. The product had low energy requirements, and sensitivity could be set at levels from ISO 100 to ISO 1600. The exposure element that had been used in digital cameras up to that point had been, for the most part, CCD sensors, but the efforts of Matsumoto and his team turned CMOS sensors into strong competitors.

Other than its use in digital cameras, the sensor was adopted for use in scanners at the lower end of the range. When a CCD sensor is used, a means of optically reducing large images is needed, but this is not required in the case of CMOS sensors. Replacement of CCD sensors by CMOS sensors made thinner scanners possible — an advantage for products designed for use in the home. Scanners with CMOS sensors are increasing Canon's market share in the popular-price zone. In addition, CMOS sensors are installed in digital x-ray cameras for medical use.

The CMOS area sensor installed in the D30 digital camera was about the same size as Advanced Photo System (APS) film, meaning that it was a little smaller than the 35mm film format that is standard for conventional negative or positive film. Matsumoto made his next target the development of a 35mm sensor. At 35mm, digital cameras could produce results that were in no way inferior to those obtained using conventional SLRs and conventional film. And if it could be used for moving images, the sensor could be adapted for use in digital video camcorders. "We're not going to outsource forever," Mitarai said. "We'll use it in strategic products such as the D30 and keep on increasing the pixel count." He was looking forward to adding to Canon's unique products.

TAKING STOCK OF TECHNOLOGY

The perseverance of engineers

Perseverance and continuity have always been the hallmarks of Canon's R&D. These qualities were certainly evident in the development of the company's electronic copying technology during the 1960s. When an electrical current is passed through a photosensitive material and toner is applied to it, an image that replicates the one that has been projected on the material is formed. If the toner can then be made to adhere to the paper, that image too can be replicated. What Canon achieved was to develop a plain-paper copier that did not infringe on patents held by Xerox, which had been the first mover in commercializing electronic copying technology. Beyond this, the company went on to introduce to the market the laser printer and the digital full-color printer.

Perseverance was behind the development of the Bubble Jet method, Canon's technique for inkjet printing. Development on this technology started in about 1976, and it took five years for the first products to reach dealers' shelves.

According to some, the discovery of Bubble Jet printing was by accident. By chance, a syringe came into contact with a soldering iron. A drop of ink squirted out from it. The episode is widely known inside and outside of the company.

The principle of the inkjet printer is to print by means of ink droplets ejected from extremely small-diameter nozzles. The goal of Ichiro Endo — now head of Technology Management Headquarters — and his development team working on Bubble Jet technology was to do so at high speed and with high quality. However, there were many problems to overcome. One problem was that the ink was getting scorched by the heat when ejected by the heat source. At engineering conferences, Canon personnel had referred to this problem as "burn". The use of black ink, basic in printing, delayed their discovery of the problem, since it didn't easily show the effects of the burning. Solving this problem was one of many that came out of a continuous process of technological research, and the accumulation of many very small advances.

Another example of how the perseverance and ingenuity of Canon's engineers have paid off can be seen in their creating of an artificial fluorite for use in camera lenses. Fluorite is an ore containing calcium fluoride in crystalline form. It has the unusual property of emitting light when heated. When used in the manufacture of camera lenses, fluorite brings a greater clarity to color and prevents a slight blurring that occurs in its absence. Canon has done development work on fluorite-enhanced lenses for 30 years, and has used fluorite for telephoto lenses made for high-end cameras. However, large crystals are required if fluorite is to have any practical application in this regard, but these are rarely found in nature. To overcome this difficulty, the company learned how to manufacture artificial crystals.

This artificial fluorite has recently been put to good use in the manufacture of semiconductors. At the end of 2001, in its work on the production of next-generation semiconductors, Canon began to use artificial-fluorite lenses to expose circuit patterns on silicon wafers. Using this technology, the company is capable of doing ultramicroscopic processing, and can make semiconductor chip circuits with line widths of 0.13 microns (one micron = one-millionth of a meter).

When Mitarai assumed the presidency in 1995, he believed that Canon's R&D had lost sight of the original objective of the company — the pursuit of profit. First, he called for the elimination of all basic research projects that showed no promise of bearing fruit over the long term. Only themes that could be made into commercial products were to be carried forward to that stage. But even when a product was introduced to the market, it would be monitored for three years. If at the end of that period there was still uncertainty about whether to continue with it, it was given an additional two years to generate a profit. If then it had still failed to become profitable, it would be dropped, regardless of the technology. "Research and development is one link in the management chain, and if it doesn't function well in that context, we eliminate it. Having continuously taken inventory of our technology, we can justify dropping anything if after three years, or five years, commercialization has not produced a profit," says Mitarai.

It was up to the top management to lop off any R&D activity that had worked its way into a dead end. That this was also good for the technical staff is evident from the cases of the PC and FLCD businesses. When Kawabata and Matsumoto were relieved of their assignments, they regained the vitality they had lost, and achieved a breakthrough by applying their technological abilities in a smarter, more productive fashion.

KICKING OFF REFORM IN RESEARCH

An hour's ride from central Tokyo, near Japan's most famous landmark, is Canon's Fuji-Susono Research Park. In the park, which commands a beautiful view of Mt. Fuji, stands the building that has been at the center of the company's work on laser printers. The facility is approached along a road that ascends gently through an area of natural beauty and is the workplace of some 1,500 people.

The building is bright and modern. The first thing the visitor sees is a luxurious lobby, behind which are the cafeteria and other parts of the research center. To enter the research lab is much like entering a library reading room. Low partitions separate an array of workstations and give the lab an air of spaciousness; the interior is coordinated in blue. A lab is often thought of as being a place of clutter and confusion, but this one is not at all like this. Desks and chairs are for common use. A researcher can use any desk and chair not already occupied and, when work is done, simply tidies up for the next person. All of the instrumentation and all of the tools are similarly shared as needed. Large pieces of equipment, such as oscilloscopes, are on trolleys; when not in use, they are wheeled back to the assigned positions.

The Five Ss

The ordered ambience at the Fuji-Susono Research Park is a result of reforms instituted and supervised by Junji Ichikawa, managing director and chief executive, Peripheral Products Operations. When Canon set up its Management Reform

Committee, including a Development System Reform Committee, Ichikawa was in charge of a task force assigned to improve the productivity of intellectual assets, and worked hard at facilitating innovation in the development process. At that time, he became aware of the disorder that prevailed in the research center, and especially in the labs. "On the production floor we adhere to the "Five Ss" rule. We have it in the development area too," says Ichikawa. The Five Ss rule is a set of principles for the workplace: *seiri* (proper arrangement); *seiso* (cleanliness); *seiton* (orderliness); *seiketsu* (neatness); and *shitsuke* (discipline). So, starting with *seiri* and *seiton*, he began by implementing this practice among the laser-printer team, of which he was in charge.

First came the big clean-up. There had been talk of cleaning up the experiment labs many times but, in the face of complaints that it would interrupt important work, nothing had ever been done. "This time, in top-down fashion, managers are going to show that they mean business. To do that we'll have every single person participate — on the basis of full understanding of why we are doing this," decided Akio Noguchi, senior general manager of the Peripherals Development Center 2. He then called in his Design Room manager and told him he wanted the entire electric experiment lab to be given a thorough cleaning. When some of the staff let it be known that they were dissatisfied with this arrangement, Noguchi adopted a hard-nosed position. Any exceptions might endanger the entire operation and would be unfair to other departments. "Just do it," he told them.

In all, the clean-up took three days and was accomplished without mishap. Then Noguchi turned his attention to improving the layout, appointing working groups charged with changing the layout of the electrical experiment lab and reforming the management of waste and consumables.

Discipline paramount

Of the Five Ss, Noguchi says, "The most important is the last, *shitsuke* (discipline). That's because if it becomes established as part of the corporate culture it all comes to be perfectly natural." To these five he added Communal Possession and Functional Beauty when establishing the concepts behind the research lab reforms. Communal Possession refers to the shared use of all tools, instruments and work space that up till then had been used on an individual basis. Every tool, every piece of equipment, was numbered and given an assigned storage place in a part of the lab called the Shop. No one was put in charge. Each person was responsible for whatever equipment they borrowed. In principle, anything was to be borrowed for one day and the rule regarding returning equipment was rigidly enforced. Working models made for test purposes too were designated as being for joint use. These models, that were custom-made by hand, ordinarily cost ¥10 million or more apiece.

Up to that time, each new employee who came to work in the development area was given a set of tools. Hand tools such as screwdrivers were considered consumable items and if one was lost the employee would simply get a replacement from General Affairs. However, when all of these were designated as communal tools, dozens appeared as if from nowhere. When an inventory of measuring instruments was taken at the time of the clean-up, duplicated instruments turned up one after another. The perennial problem of there never being enough low-voltage power sources, for example, was eliminated instantly. In the case of items such as screwdrivers and soldering irons, it became possible for eight or so to be sufficient for the needs of 40 people. With more costly instruments, such as oscilloscopes, which could cost as much as ¥8 million, one proved to be sufficient.

Work space too was made communal. Two types of space were made; one for individual study, similar to the carrel area in a library, and one for joint study, for when a development team had to work together. Joint-study areas took on the appearance of clusters formed around working models. Redundant items were taken away, and space requirements were reduced — just as they had been tightened on the production floor. Now, there was space to spare.

Functional Beauty meant, in essence, easy to use and easy on the eye. It wasn't simply a case of relying on the clean-up to improve appearances. When shelves, desks, other office furniture and the like were purchased, functional beauty was adopted as a criterion. After the clean-up, Ichikawa picked up terms used in figure-skating competitions, and used them for monthly evaluations. He gave scores for "artistic conception" and for "technical points". "I scored from one to five; five was a perfect performance and three was a pass. The research park passed easily," Ichikawa said. "The only question was whether it could be sustained."

Ichikawa extended what Noguchi had started in the electrical experiment lab to cover the entire Fuji-Susono Research Park. When, in April 2001, another laser-printer development team was brought in from Toride and elsewhere, Ichikawa took it as an opportunity to fastidiously review the layout of the entire research facility using the same basic principles.

Early detection by middle management

The spate of reforms enabled the Fuji-Susono Research Park to slash its annual equipment budget by more than 60%. The space that had been made available could accommodate a moderate increase in the staff. The use of communal working models was particularly significant. At Ichikawa's suggestion, Noguchi and his team had taken photos of how things were before the clean-up. They show just how greatly things have changed. The photos are being kept for future generations of workers as evidence of how things were before.

As had happened with the production reforms at Nagahama and other factories, the workforce in the research park contributed to the changes by introducing changes that improved efficiency in the labs. Who better to introduce housekeeping changes than the housekeepers themselves?

But the most important advantage of the reforms, Noguchi says, was that they gave engineers more time to do their thinking. By making the location of tools and equipment fixed and evident, preparation time for experiments was greatly reduced. "Things probably wouldn't have gone well from the outset if there had been a bottom-up procedure. It was the top-down sequence that changed awareness," says Masahide Chino, general manager of the Peripherals Development Strategy Management Center. What Chino means by top-down is leadership by middle management. Managers come in at 8:30, before work starts, to check conditions in the labs and, if there are problems, they give the staff whatever instructions are needed. The incidence of problems has fallen recently but this arrangement is continuing.

One more matter troubled Ichikawa and Noguchi. While it is important for engineers to have a free environment in which to express their creativity best, there were glaring examples of the misuse of that freedom. Symbolic of this was the way engineers dressed. There was no dress code in the development departments, and some employees were wearing sandals when they greeted visitors or were walking about with shirttails out. Ichikawa and others drew up a dress code, announcing it in September 1999 as being applicable to all employees at the research park. The rules called for everyone to wear a prescribed jacket and forbade the wearing of jeans.

That September, Mitarai visited the Fuji-Susono Research Park. Although his objective, ostensibly, was to see firsthand the results of the reforms, what he and Ichikawa were aiming at was leveraging the visit to spread the reform movement to all groups. Mitarai commended the research park for breaking the ice and called for the company to learn from Susono. After this visit, the top people and managers at other operating divisions visited the research park; more than a hundred of them came in the space of just two months. As a result, the divisions in charge of chemical products, copying machines and cameras began to reform their research facilities.

DOUBLING THE NUMBER OF PRODUCTS

Digital photography was a new business area that Mitarai believed to be promising. The iPrinter Development Center was responsible for the design of inkjet printers, the core of the company's digital-photo business. By coupling digital cameras and printers and eliminating the traditional process of developing film, the digital-photo system allows photos to be enjoyed at home. As a result of this technology, by 2001 the iPrinter Development Center was able to develop twice as many products as it had two years earlier, but with no change in the number of employees. The center succeeded in cutting the cost of studies for working models of products by two-thirds, and reduced the interdepartmental failure cost during product development, also by two-thirds, over a three-year period. While it is difficult to quantify productivity in the development area, it certainly can be stated that the effectiveness of development was substantially improved.

One way in which Canon was able to accomplish this was through a three-pronged approach combining the Knowledge Intensive system (KI), 3D computer-aided design and quality engineering. "Combining quality engineering, KI and 3D computer-aided design doubles development capability," says Atsushi Noda, a division head at the iPrinter Development Center, explaining the results of his own development innovation. What, then, are the three tools that the iPrinter Development Center used to accomplish its development reforms?

The Taguchi method

Quality engineering is a specific term also known as the "Taguchi method" after the engineer who developed it, Genichi Taguchi, who was inducted into the Automotive Hall of Fame in the United States in 1997 and into the Hall of Fame for Engineering, Science and Technology in 1998. The use of quality engineering is a method of reducing variations in quality in the manufacture of technology; that is, it is a systematic way to improve overall quality.

KI: Organized pandemonium

KI activities refer to work undertaken in accordance with a Knowledge Intensive Staff Innovation Plan, a method developed by JMA Consultants, a major consulting firm in Tokyo. The objective of such a plan is the smooth functioning of the project team working on the development of a particular new product. For example, in order to ensure good communication within the team from the initial phase of development, a meeting called a "Technology Disclosure" is held. Technology Disclosure meetings analyze in detail the technology required for the new product that is to be developed. At these meetings, everyone present can talk openly. The environment of unrestrained freedom is one that has been called *waiwaigayagaya*, which translates as "organized pandemonium". JMAC borrowed the term from Honda Motor. With help from JMAC, Noda and his staff began implementing KI in 1999. It was first employed for a three-year project to develop a new laser printer and involved a project team of around 50 people.

At the Technology Disclosure meeting, all the issues at hand were reviewed. On that basis, a Strategy Story was compiled, and a time schedule was drawn up. This schedule, following the overall plan, was broken down into weekly units and outlined what each person had to do in any particular week. Each issue was written on a slip of paper and the slips were glued to large sheets of vellum board.

A KI Room was set aside at the Tamagawa Plant where development work on inkjet printers was concentrated, and the vellum display boards were put up so that all team members could see them. Training in use of the KI technique lasted one year.

While adopting KI for this three-year project, in 2000 Canon also decided to use it for a one-year project involving a new product. The one-year project, according to Noda, was to validate the essence of KI and the manner of its use was modified. All project staff participated in the Technology Disclosure meeting, and the subsequent checking of progress was done by individual design teams, each of which had an average of 10 members.

The project in question was to design a product of strategic importance for digital-photo operations. Given the brand name "Pixus" in Japan, it was a direct-print inkjet printer — meaning that it could be connected directly to compatible digital cameras to print photos — which included among its features high-speed printing, high image quality and quiet operation. At the Technology Disclosure meeting, discussion centered on how to combat a rival company's similar product that could produce borderless "edge-to-edge" prints, and how to keep the new product quiet when printing at high speed. Each of these issues was assigned to a design team, their schedules were made, and vellum sheets with slips of paper attached were posted.

There was no magical remedy for reducing noise. It was necessary to use routine approaches, by investigating the effects of adopting various materials, and of using different structural designs. Diligent application of the KI method eventually enabled Canon's engineers to achieve high-speed operation without the usual by-product of a high noise level.

The first person to take note of KI activities was Kunio Watanabe, group executive, Corporate Strategy & Development Headquarters. "Japanese companies," he says, "now suffer from insufficient three-way cooperation." He was referring here to a lack of communication between research and development, production and marketing, and to the walls built between these divisions. Watanabe believes that there should be more consolidated management. "In Japan at this time, there is surprisingly little dialogue between managers and younger employees. The barstool conferences of the old days are gone and the use of email is eroding personal interaction. Canon is no exception," he says.

Having learned about it at a JMAC lecture in late 1998, Watanabe saw KI as a means of improving vertical communication at the workplace, and a means of smoothing the development process. When Watanabe mentioned KI in the company, it was the inkjet printer people who were the first to show interest and to use it. As Watanabe sees it, beyond creating an atmosphere where everyone brought their own knowledge into the discussion, KI was a wake-up call for middle management, which had grown complacent. KI activities made it possible to track the progress of a project, and to know at a glance where the burden was greatest. It also provided input for decisions regarding the allocation of staff. Moreover, it prevented middle management from using the old practice of conveying instructions by giving a vague indication of what the boss wanted. "Setting priorities and mobilizing the available brainpower to resolve problems is where management shows its abilities," says Noda. KI becomes a tryout ground for managers. Plans call for expanding its use to cover development projects for laser printers and cameras.

Improving communication using 3D CAD

Three-dimensional computer-aided design (3D CAD) is a system for representing three-dimensional objects as images on computer monitors. These images are far, far better than the two-dimensional images on paper that had previously been the standard products of CAD. No special expertise is needed to view and use these images. The iPrinter Development Center was the epicenter for KI activities but not for 3D CAD. Canon lacks infrastructure for designing things and for developing them, according to Mitarai. He therefore advocated to the Management Reform Committee that 3D CAD be adopted at an early time, as a standard-bearer for innovation and change. Selection and planning for this was begun in 1998.

3D CAD empowers the process of communication with people outside of the design area. While the designers may well believe that they have turned out a good design, the marketing personnel, who are closer to the consumers and end users, may be of the opinion that the design is behind the times. In order to eliminate these post-design problems, presentations are now held from the outset with the heads of production, sales, business planning, quality assurance, and safety standards departments. All of them can voice their opinions. If potential problems can be identified in advance, redesign costs can be greatly reduced.

Up until that point, the iPrinter Development Center had been using 3D CAD for presentations to some departments, but not to the design department. So, at the Tamagawa Plant, one room was set aside specifically for presentations and equipped with a large screen to show 3D CAD images. It has telecommunications links to production facilities in Japan and Thailand. The appearance and other characteristics of products under development can be readily seen and understood without requiring specialized knowledge of design, thus enabling an increasing number of employees in business operations and planning areas to provide their opinions and comments. As a result, the amount of redesign work required is declining. Another advantage of CAD is that it simplifies processes that used to entail highly specialized calculations, so that the work can now be performed by whoever is doing the design work.

Use of 3D CAD had been adopted by all development departments by the end of 2000, and its use is continuing to spread in the actual work outside of the i Printer Development Center — in camera, copier and other development areas.

Where KI activities develop middle-management abilities, and 3D CAD improves inter-departmental communication, quality engineering enhances the powers of engineers. Each of the three tools yields a different effect. The combination of the three embodies Canon's approach to development.

HAVING AND USING KEY TECHNOLOGY: WORKING TOGETHER AS A FAMILY

Since its founding, Canon has had a closeness that is usually only found in families. The company has always provided the kind of environment in which its engineers and technical staff can share their expertise in working together as circumstances dictate. The effectiveness of this approach was clearly evident in the development of the Bubble Jet method for inkjet printers. The idea for a heat source required for these machines came from a team then working on a micro heater for heat-sensitive paper used in calculators. They enabled the heater to be attached around the nozzles that ejected the ink by a process called sputtering, a technology that had already been used for making thermal heads for printing on heat-sensitive paper.

This approach is continuing to improve. The basic technology being developed in various departments can be freely accessed by researchers and engineers from other departments, so that technology circulates within the company. Inhouse technology that can be shared, referred to internally as "element technology", was born of necessity and the sharing process has evolved gradually into its present form. Major components that have been made by using element technology are called "key components". The combination of element technology and key components is referred to as "key tech".

THE DIGITAL CAMERA TURNAROUND

Canon's digital camera operations have been doing well. Camera sales in 2003 amounted to ¥654 billion, on a consolidated basis, up 35% year on year. Traditional film cameras are mature products and showed almost no growth, so almost all of the growth is attributable to digital cameras. Canon is one

Key Technology	
KEY COMPONENTS	**ELEMENT TECHNOLOGY**
NADA, CMOS sensors image engines	Bubble Jet technology, nanoprocessing technology, digital imaging technology, optical technology

of the world's four largest digital camera makers, along with Sony, Fuji and Olympus.

The reason for the strong performance is the Ixus (Elph in the U.S. market) series of digital cameras. When the first Ixus digital camera was introduced in May 2000, it did well in the market as it was the smallest and lightest of its class then available and at once became the top-selling model. The Ixus cameras sported a stainless-steel exterior that imparted the same feeling given by high-end cameras, and were flat enough to slip easily into a pocket. Before this product, Canon's digital camera operations had been little more than a shadow of Fuji's.

The Digital Ixus i (PowerShot SD10 Digital Elph in the U.S. market) lineup, available in four color variations, launched in October 2003

Behind the realization of this new design was a key technology called the "image engine", a semiconductor chip about 13 mm square which performed all of the functions needed for a digital camera. The circuitry for processing signals thus was greatly reduced in size, enabling the entire camera to be smaller and lighter.

In developing the image engine, a stream of difficulties had to be overcome. The story of developing the image engine begins in an earlier period when electronics was being applied to still cameras for the first time.

Digital cameras take images through the conversion of light into digital signals by a CCD image sensor, and the image is recorded not on silver halide film but in a magnetic memory medium. This was first done in still cameras but the method of making a magnetic record was analog, not digital. Sony was the first to develop such a product, the Mavica, which was brought to market in 1981. Intent on coming up with a competing product, Canon undertook development work that led to the commercialization of a still video camera, the RC-701, in 1986. Other manufacturers of electrical appliances and cameras had came up with a number of prototypes, but Canon's RC-701 was the first that reached production.

An electronic camera that did not require film was heralded as the camera of the future. The high price, however, prevented it from being a successful mainstream product. The retail price of the RC-701 was ¥390,000 or about US$3,000. The RC-760, launched in 1988, was priced at ¥590,000. At that price, however, the market was extremely limited. Canon went ahead with developing a model that could be sold to the general public and, in September 1989, brought out the RC-250, named Q-PIC in Japan and ION in Europe, with a price tag of ¥98,000. Q-PIC had built-in playback capability, so connecting it to a video monitor via a cable made it easy to display images. Sales in Europe were sufficient for it to be considered a hit there, but in Japan they did not reach the expected level. Subsequently, in 1992, Canon introduced the high-grade RC-570, which marked the end of its development of electronic still cameras.

Yukichi Niwa, who had been at the Canon Research Center and is now head of the Platform Technology Development

Canon engineers working on next-generation display technology at the Canon Research Center in Japan

Headquarters, moved about 60 of his team to work on video camcorders and high-speed copiers. The remaining 140 were assigned to developing digital cameras. The Photo Products Group at the time was not performing well, as growth of compact-camera sales had petered out, and this situation made the division a little wary of the development of a digital camera. It was Niwa who moved the development out into the Peripheral Products Group, which had among its products laser printers and computer-related equipment.

Developing the image engine

Having taken a strong hit with the failure in electronic still cameras, the development team was favorably disposed towards any new assignment. Mitarai was greatly interested in digital cameras, and encouraged them, but there were others in the company who were unconvinced that his interest held potential. This was the environment in which Niwa came up with the concept of the image engine.

A computer would be built into the digital camera, to control its operation and to provide an improved output image. If this could be achieved with a single chip, it would remove three problems at once, by making the camera lighter, smaller and cheaper to produce. It was evident enough that if the number of chips could be reduced to one, and it wasn't necessary to have the circuitry on a large board, the camera would be small and light. Beyond that, however, was the promise of lower unit costs that would be achieved by high-volume production of that chip. Functionality too would be improved, as advances in semiconductor processing technology suggested that a more complex circuit than had been used in the past could be used on the chip.

In early-generation digital cameras, Canon used a chip that was a modified version of the one used in video camcorders. About seven semiconductors had been used in combination, and finding a way to reduce this to just one presented formidable difficulties. Not least of these was the fact that it then took three years to develop a special-purpose chip. And it would take much longer if a different chip was needed for each new model of digital camera. Compression of the camera's digital image was a demanding process, and required that the chip be able to perform high-speed functions. Moreover, in order to enable lengthy periods of use running on battery, the chip had to consume very little energy. All of these pointed to the need for a new chip.

At this time, Niwa thought of splitting the digital camera's functions into separate parts. One was for general control — control of the transmission of image data, file management, and so on — and another for control of the image signal processing — in other words, an image engine. To achieve the former, it would be sufficient to tweak semiconductor chips already on the market. Image-taking control, however, would require expertise in the field of optical technology, which Canon had. Rather than try to combine both functions on one chip, Niwa decided two chips would greatly shorten development time and, at the same time, improve functionality.

Work on modifying a chip for general control was started, making use of recent developments in semiconductor technology. Meanwhile, if Canon's proprietary technology could be adapted for the image-taking control, little work would be needed for the second chip. Canon could make refinements to meet the required changes — such as the increase in the number of pixels of the CCD (charged couple device, a light-sensitive chip that is the digital camera's "eye"). The image-control chip became Canon's image engine.

Niwa worked out the concept of the image engine with the development team. In the meantime, the company introduced a compact digital camera, the PowerShot 600, in July 1996. This had a suggested retail price of ¥128,000.

But in the preceding year, Casio, a rival company known primarily for its calculators, had delivered its QV-10 liquid-crystal digital camera, with the shockingly low price of ¥65,000. It was a big hit and Canon was left behind. The QV-10 did not have the image quality that a camera-maker would offer to consumers but broke new ground by being sold as a fun product, good for taking snapshots at parties or at similar occasions. What was special about the QV-10, apart from the price, was a small liquid-crystal panel in the back, where the most recent image recorded could be viewed. With a simplicity that outdid the Polaroid cameras, it was an overnight success. Casio kept it up; in March 1996 they brought out the QV-10A, priced at less than ¥50,000, and market demand surged for the product.

A sense of danger

While all this was going on, Canon's development staff began to feel a sense of danger. Early in 1996 the employees charged with developing digital cameras were split off from Peripheral Products Operations and made a part of product development. At the time, Product Development Operations had a mandate to develop the seeds of strategically important future products, using the project-team approach. And at the same time, other groups which were short of technical staff adept at digital work tried to raid product development. The development team was on the verge of coming apart at the seams.

Niwa approached Mitarai, telling him, "If things go on as they now are, all my good engineers will be scattered across the company. Can't you do something?" This was in the autumn of 1996. Mitarai's reaction was to place the digital-camera development team under his direct control because of the importance of digital cameras to the company's future.

The name of the newly reassigned unit was the Digital Imaging Business Center. In January 1997, Niwa was named as its head. Working directly under the president, Niwa used the occasion to start real work on the image engine. "There was still opposition from within the company about allocating money and resources to developing digital cameras, which were not making it as a commercial product," says Niwa.

In July 1998 Mitarai decided to relocate the digital camera team to the Photo Products Group (today's Image Communication Headquarters). He combined his team with the camera development team under Tsuneji Uchida, currently senior managing director and running the Image Communication Headquarters, and all went to work on developing a completely new digital camera, one that would fully exploit the potential of the image engine.

For the digital camera team this meant more pressure. They had led a privileged existence when it was the president who was in charge of their group. Not only were they now reduced to ordinary-citizen status in the Photo Products Group, they had to shoulder responsibility for making a direct contribution to a successful product. The group released top-of-the-line digital SLR cameras, the EOS D2000 and EOS D6000, in 1998, as well as the cheaper PowerShot A5 and PowerShot Pro 70. Consumer reaction was lukewarm. There was no change in Canon's lowly position in the digital camera market. The need to turn the situation around, by bringing out an entirely new model based on an innovative technology, was now even greater than ever.

"Canon was accused of being uninterested in digital cameras — which made us that much more intent on accomplishing something," says Masaya Maeda, who had worked on digital camera development, and is now deputy group executive of the Digital Imaging Business Group in the Image Communication Products Operations. What brought smiles to faces in the digital camera R&D lab was the appearance of the Digital Ixus (Digital Elph in the U.S. market) compact camera. "If we can come up with a model this size, we'll have a winner," Maeda thought.

The goal was to sell a digital camera with about two megapixels for about ¥50,000, one developed by Uchida and Kazuya Hosoe, now senior managing director of Image Communication Products Operations. They believed that two megapixels would be enough for viewing images the size of those taken with an ordinary compact camera. They planned on overtaking their competitors by relying on new technology, such as the image engine. They would give it a small Ixus-like body, making it smaller than existing digital cameras.

Flooring the accelerator

The image-engine concept evolved into its final form and, in mid 1998, a prototype was built, with a view to rolling out the new product in the spring of 2001. However, Maeda and his workers suggested that they could get it to market ahead of schedule and the roll-out was moved forward to 2000. Behind this decision was Mitarai's strong interest in having a product ready for the dawn of the new millennium.

The image engine was completed in 1999. Its first uses were for the PowerShot S10 and S20, which would hit the market in autumn that year. According to Uchida, however, they ran into trouble while developing the chip for general camera control. An improved image engine was installed in the Digital Ixus 200 and 300 models in 2001. The new engine was able to process at higher speeds and give better image quality than its predecessor. The Digital Ixus 300 is capable of processing two megapixels in just 0.4 seconds. It plays back images and sound with relative ease. In addition to being capable of processing signals on the basis of an algorithm optimized for a primary color filter for better image quality, it draws much less power from batteries than its predecessor did.

The reasons behind the success of Digital Ixus cameras are their small size, their light weight and their chic appearance. The image engine was the primary factor enabling it to be small and light, but Uchida offers another reason: the "one-yen" lens.

A series of lens elements are combined to make up the lens unit of a camera, and for these Ixus models the overall cross-section of the entire lens system spanned only 20mm, or less than the diameter of a Japanese one-yen coin. Optical systems account for relatively large parts of cameras. Unless the lens component can be made small, the camera can't easily be reduced in size. The target for the Digital Ixus cameras was a body depth of 25mm. The result was a thickness of 26.9mm. It was the one-yen lens that enabled Canon to almost attain its goal.

The one-yen lens in the first-generation Ixus cameras had a 2× zoom capability but the Digital Ixus 300 had an optical system that had a 3× capacity. The lens diameter was increased slightly but it became possible to improve the zoom ratio with almost no change in the size of the camera body. This was a remarkable improvement.

Canon's characteristic style in developing new products is to always embody key technology in which new "element

The 6.3 megapixel EOS 300D Digital (EOS Digital Rebel in the U.S. market)

technology" and a key component are combined. Canon's insistence on proprietary products derives from its insistence on having proprietary key components. Plain-paper copiers, laser printers, Bubble Jet printers — all conform to this. They were developed in an atmosphere wherein high importance was assigned to key technology. Because the development of key technology and the development of a new product often proceed together, it is inevitable that the process takes a certain amount of time. And when competition with other companies gets intense, any delay in the development process can prove costly.

The development of the image engine contains the germ of a new method, which was the key technology for the Digital Ixus cameras. Development of the key technology went first, and then was used in a variety of digital cameras. The image engine was also used in digital SLR cameras. This particular key technology was embodied in many different products so that the technology was circulated within the company. It is also possible to develop several versions or types of product. The improved image engine can be used in the PowerShot series, which is expected to be at the core of Canon's digital camera business. Moreover, the concept is also applicable to copiers and inkjet printers.

In 2001, Niwa took up his current post of group executive of the Platform Technology Development Headquarters. The name of this part of the company was provided by Niwa, with the intention of having this department serve as a platform for key technology such as the image engine.

NEW KEY TECHNOLOGY FOR COPIERS

If Canon is likened to a stout tree, the trunk is the business of supplying copiers for business use. There, digital technology is in the process of taking over.

Canon was a bit behind rival makers Ricoh and Xerox in digitizing copiers, a fact acknowledged by Ikuo Soma, who heads the Office Imaging Products Operations. "There's no denying that we were slow in digitizing monochrome copiers and developing our product series," he says. "This was influenced by the continuing strong sales of analog machines in the U.S. market." The means by which the company sought to catch up was by introducing a new lineup of digital multifunctional copiers, the imageRUNNER (iR) series. This was in July 2000.

Copying machines, fundamentally, are scanners and printers combined. But digitizing makes it possible for the machines to be equipped with additional functions. A filing function is one example. The idea is to place business documents into the copier's memory, from which they can be retrieved as hard copy when needed. As long as the document has been digitized, doing a search is easy and filing is much simpler than handling paper. Copiers in the series were also capable of being linked to a network to facilitate access to documents.

But even if Canon endowed the machine with multifunctionality, the company couldn't be certain how the machines would actually be used. A filing function, after all, is inherent in computers, from which documents can be printed on demand. To build a network, computers alone could suffice. There was thus some anxiety over the possibility that a multiple of functions could mean too many functions.

Despite these thoughts, the first imageRUNNER machine to be released, the iR3250, was loaded with all the functions — sending email messages, sending documents to fax machines, scanning material up to A3 size, a document-management system, temporary storage of large quantities of data, remote control by a personal computer, and so on. "Usually we work toward limiting the functions we offer. But in this case,

Canon's imageRUNNER C3200 color, networked, digital, multi-function office system

we took the opposite approach. The iR3250 was sent to the market to survey it, and depending on the reactions of users, we would make new decisions on which functions to keep and which to eliminate," says Soma. Canon subsequently eliminated email and fax functions in later iR6000 models.

Digital printers require more than printer engines and scanner engines that embody mechanical and electric technology; they also must have electronic devices such as controllers that regulate overall functioning.

NADA, which had been developed by Kawabata and his co-workers at the Platform Technology Development Headquarters, was used in the imageRUNNER series and is a classic example of this. It is expected that there will be further use of such key technology in developing new digital copiers.

There is one more key technology for digital copiers: the software. Soma emphasizes that development of the software for document management alone is half of the work. Canon calls the software it develops for digital copiers "imageware". The first time such software became available was in October 2001. The idea was that a limited version of imageware would be offered free of charge, and it would generate income flow when functions were expanded. It can be said that improving the software further, and establishing it as a key technology, is a challenge for the future.

Plain-paper copiers and laser printers employ the same key technology of electrophotography. Optical technology that was first applied in cameras was in time exploited as a key technology for steppers. Sharing or circulating technology within the company is a tradition at Canon. Recently, however, Canon has started to develop key technology and develop new products separately from one another. Rather than proceed from the development of key technology to the development of products, staff engaged in product development proceed with their work while keeping tabs on key technology development. When they see something they can use, they bring it in. In the days when product development extended over a period of three years, it was acceptable for both development processes to proceed in tandem. But product life cycles have become shorter, making it necessary to greatly condense the development phase, to the extent that it is no longer feasible to wait for the development of key technology. It was the scanner team that was first to adopt the tandem-development arrangement, when they worked on a popularly priced scanner.

Scanning new horizons

About 40 people were at work on developing a reasonably priced scanner. Even though there was a great difference in market scale, this was a puny force compared to the 1,500 personnel assigned to develop laser printers at the Fuji-Susono Research Park. "Even when we increased the number of models to be developed, we didn't increase the number of personnel," says Katsuichi Shimizu, former deputy chief executive of Office Imaging Products Operations, who is now chief executive of Inkjet Products Operations.

Though Japanese companies had developed and made the first scanners, they soon came under pressure from manufacturers from the United States, Europe, Taiwan and elsewhere. The low-price strategy of the Taiwanese makers was audacious. Their retail prices in the United States were below Canon's production costs but, Shimizu found, the profit ratio of the Taiwanese makers was between 5% and 10% of sales. Seeing this, he hit upon the idea of asking Taiwanese manufacturers to supply their products to be sold under the Canon brand.

He was surprised to see the differences between the Taiwanese companies' parts, assembly, management and profits and those that existed in Japan. For the Taiwanese, for example, the cost of glass was one-fifth that in Japan.

Buying from OEMs, however, brought a problem of quality. Quality is largely determined by design, which involves both specifications and the preparation of engineering drawings. So Canon made designs and asked the Taiwanese companies to produce according to those designs. Canon set things up so that it was responsible for both the beginning and end processes, by doing the overall design and undertaking quality assurance after the Taiwanese companies had completed the engineering drawings and production. For a time, this manner of contract manufacturing went well.

But personnel costs in Taiwan eventually began to rise and Canon countered this by building a plant in Zhuhai, China. Because labor costs were much lower than in Taiwan, production shifted to the mainland. Canon would buy semiconductors, critical parts for scanners, in Taiwan, and have other parts made in China. At the time of writing, Canon was having design work done in Taiwan but it is highly possible that soon this too will be moved to China. China, anticipating this shift, has begun to develop its engineering capacity.

Overall design by Canon, engineering in Taiwan, manufacturing in China: this is the present pattern for Canon's scanner operations. Many of the 69 companies that had been in the scanner business in June 1997 had been forced out, and as of 2001 only six companies were still making scanners.

KEY TECHNOLOGY: HIDDEN TREASURES

"In the scanner business," Shimizu says, "[having] a global brand is of the greatest importance." At the same time that prices were being kept as low as possible through control of production and distribution costs, sales would make use of branding power to move the goods through the sales network. This is a classic business model, applicable to personal computers and reasonably priced digital equipment. Shimizu set to work at adopting a build-to-order system such as that used by Dell Computer, whereby the company would not have to carry inventory. Parts vendors supplying the Zhuhai plant in China were situated close to the Canon factory and could deliver parts in a manner that was akin to the Just-in-Time system. How to improve distribution was the major challenge.

Even if adopting a build-to-order scheme meant that the company would be no worse than its competitors, this alone did not provide enough strength for it to be any better. Exploiting key technology to make products that were uniquely Canon's was the way to achieve superior competitiveness. But there wasn't enough freedom to let a 40-person development team concentrate on R&D for key technology.

Shimizu thought that there must be resources in the company, somewhere, that he could draw upon. He started looking for key technology he could use in scanners. When he discovered the CMOS sensor that Shigeyuki Matsumoto's team had developed, he had found what he was looking for. This sensor enabled Canon to launch a scanner in 1998 that was slimmer than any of the competitors'.

Another move was the use of dormant patents. If film is exposed to infrared light, microscopic particles of dust can be detected. This technology was patented as long ago as 1986. When the sensitivity of scanners was improved, they too revealed the microscopic dust particles, which appeared on the image as black specks. Thereupon a system was developed using the patented technology that could "ignore" such tiny particles. This system was used in some new scanner models introduced in 2001.

The scanner development team did not give this patent any attention at the outset. An American venture company approached Canon, offering to sell it essentially the same technology, and Canon started to consider this as a business proposition. As a matter of routine, a check was made of the company's own patents, and it was found that the same technology had already been developed. No doubt Canon has many more examples of sleeping technology that it can put to good advantage.

The 3M company uses the technology-platform concept in order to use inhouse key technology in its various departments. The idea is to develop technology as a platform that can be used by as many parts of the company as possible. At Canon a platform is vitally important in areas such as scanners, where development must be exceptionally rapid. Yet, at the same time, the company is working at developing key technology for specific targets, such as the CMOS sensor, NADA and the image engine. It is clear from the name of Kawabata's division — the Platform Technology Development Headquarters — that Canon has begun to embrace the technology-platform concept. In addition, Phase II of Canon's Excellent Global Corporation Plan, a five-year management initiative that was kicked off in 2001, calls for "development of key components, including both hardware and software, and strengthening the company's basic, company-wide technology." But in actuality there are many parts of the company where the advances are spontaneous events rather than the result of deliberate actions with a concrete goal.

Managing for total optimization of technology

Canon's basic strategy is to achieve innovation through proprietary technology, and use that technology to open up new markets. "We always use technology as our base, and enter industries that have been derived from that technology. While always depending on our own technology, we add to it and enter new industries by that route. We've diversified, and sought higher levels of value added. It has been a management strategy founded on technology," says Mitarai. What has not changed since the company was established is the fact that Canon has been oriented towards research and development that links creative research with new products.

RESEARCH THAT GENERATES CASH

If, nevertheless, technological development ends up as just a series of individual success stories, or simply cultivates a sense of self-importance, it will not lead to improved competitiveness. If it doesn't generate more revenue for Canon in overall terms, it has no meaning at all. No matter how good the researchers, no matter how good the engineers, it is essential that concrete results be obtained from their development work. Even if research yields good results, unless it can be made into a product, it is nothing more than a white elephant. Unless the product can be sold, no income can be secured.

The inexpensive product that lies in the company's warehouses because it can't be sold is best left unmade. If optimization is achieved only in the production area, the overall cash flow will not improve. In the same way, as graphic as the development results may be, if the product made possible by that development can't be sold and becomes "inventory", the development investment becomes a loss. When researchers and engineers suffer a drop in morale and fritter away time at useless R&D, this is little more than an unwanted build-up of inventory. By making thoroughgoing, effective use of internal resources, R&D personnel increase the value of the company's cash flow. This is the meaning of Mitarai's "managing for total optimization of technology."

Movement in this direction has already begun. The first steps were taken soon after Mitarai took the helm, when the company announced that it would quit unprofitable business areas, and when R&D activities were subjected to close scrutiny and analysis. Since the Management Reform Committee was set up in 1998, R&D reform has been a major topic, together with production reform. Each of the package of improvements — at the labs at Fuji-Susono Research Park, the KI activities, and the use of 3D CAM in the entire R&D area — was undertaken with the conscious thought of forging another link in a chain of development innovation. Mitarai's intentions lay behind all of this.

Production reform was embodied in the switch to the cell system. Though great strides have been made, development reform is, by comparison, still groping for direction.

In April 1996, a Product Development Headquarters was added to the existing R&D Headquarters as the development units directly attached to the head office. While the R&D Headquarters was in charge of basic research, the Product Development Operations was organized to undertake development of the technology that could prove to be the seeds of new businesses. In addition, the Camera Operations unit had within it a Video Products Development Center, and the Office Imaging Products Operations had within it the Office Imaging Products Development Center. Each had staff dedicated to improving existing products and other development tasks.

This all changed in July 1999. The R&D Headquarters and the Product Development Operations were eliminated and in their place Canon established a Technology Management Headquarters, a Core Technology Development Headquarters, a Platform Development Headquarters, a Display Development Headquarters, an Internet Business Development Headquarters, and an Operations Promotion Headquarters. In 2001, a Device Development Headquarters was added to these six.

Broadly speaking, three of these — the Technology Management Headquarters, the Core Technology Development Headquarters, and the Platform Development Headquarters — work at basic research, while the others work at development aimed at the creation of new products and new business. For example, the Canon Research Center is part of the Core Technology Development Headquarters. Similarly, the CMOS sensor (the "eye" of the digital camera) and the SOI (the next-generation semiconductor wafer) are being developed at Device Development Headquarters. The Display Development Headquarters is working on the SED flat-panel displays. NADA, the control element in copiers, however, falls within the domain of the Platform Development Headquarters. This is perhaps a consequence of the company having to be flexible in adapting to the rapid pace of technological change.

The Bubble Jet i990 inkjet printer delivers photo-quality prints and enables users to print out directly from a digital camera

AWAITING THE BLOCKBUSTER

One vital issue remains. There has been no blockbuster product equal to the Bubble Jet printer to come out of Canon since the 1990s. Searching for a niche for proprietary technology, where patents can be protected, is traditional at Canon. But the copier market is not like that of basic industries such as automobiles and steel, which operate on a much larger scale and whose products are sold throughout the world. Watanabe, at Corporate Strategy & Development Headquarters, calls this a "global niche". The formula for victory at Canon is to identify this kind of market where the company's proprietary technology can be exploited. Although there have been some successes, such as with the digital camera, strong performance has not been recorded on a sustained basis.

If a powerful product can be brought to market, morale in the company will soar, along with its global reputation. Of course, when this happens, business performance also improves. If a link can be achieved between managing for total optimization of technology and a big hit product, this would give the company even more market muscle.

What Canon really needs is a blockbuster product. Recognizing this, Mitarai's response has been to invest heavily in R&D, mergers and acquisitions, and business alliances, to bring outside technology into the company. During the three years starting in 2001 the company would invest a total of ¥1 trillion, or about US$833 million, in R&D, M&A and new businesses through alliances. Of this sum, ¥800 billion would go for R&D for Canon and ¥200 billion would be for M&A. The composition of R&D investment would be of the order of 300 billion for regular R&D, 300 billion for SED flat-panel displays and other new products, 100 billion for products such as digital cameras, and the remaining 100 billion for long-term R&D. This three-year R&D investment plan represents a 67% increase over the three-year period up to 2000.

Canon would look for opportunities primarily in the U.S. for M&A. In the summer of 1999 an inhouse M&A team was formed in Canon U.S.A. A director at the parent company, Toru Takahashi, was selected to serve as senior vice president of Canon U.S.A. and identify suitable M&A opportunities in the United States.

"From now on, our strengths are going to be in images, in telecommunications, in electronics and in chemicals. In what we call Canon-style multimedia, we intend to provide the equipment for digital networks for the home and for the office," says Mitarai.

Candidates for blockbuster status have already emerged. First off, there are "the three Ss": the SED; the System on a Chip; and SOI for making semiconductors. To these can be added the CMOS sensor. There are also possibilities of new markets, of hybrid products such as the combination used in the digital-photo technologies.

There is no denying that the company lacks experience in M&A and other methods of acquiring new technology from outside. It is not going to be easy to come up with a winner.

4

Unchanged at the Core

MITARAI SPEAKS

As soon as he took over as president and CEO in 1995, Mitarai set out at once to promote American-style reforms through top-down management. He immediately took the company out of non-profitable lines and within two years had completed the introduction of the cell-production method at domestic factories. And yet, despite a groundswell of opinion among Japanese managers that there should be greater mobility of human resources in industry, he held fast to the Japanese tradition of lifelong employment. He believed that a lifelong-employment system brought a sense of cohesion to the workforce, giving employees a sense of common destiny and the company greater competitiveness. But he dispensed with the seniority system, preferring to implement a thoroughgoing scheme of meritocracy. The coexistence of lifetime employment and meritocracy is the keynote of Mitarai's management philosophy.

The following is an explication of this philosophy, prepared on the basis of several interviews.

The advantages of lifetime employment

Q: *What are your reasons for preferring the practice of lifetime employment?*

M: The real core of the company is its employees. Without them, the company doesn't exist. If you think about the question of what the real strength of a company is, it is the strength of its employees. Train the employees and they become invigorated. When employees apply themselves diligently, they will advance towards a common goal, powered by the sense of sharing a destiny. In Japan, this is encapsulated in the form of the lifetime-employment arrangement. In a demanding managerial environment, having a small talented crew bound together by a common purpose and a sense of common destiny is vastly superior to an organization that is formed and dispersed primarily on the basis of monetary motives. This is very much where Canon's resources originate.

The advantage of lifelong employment is that the employee acquires lifelong understanding of the management policies and corporate culture. Protection of the brand and devotion to the company are formidable intangible assets, since competing against other companies is a confrontation of one organization against another. In my opinion, it both matches the Japanese social environment and constitutes a core competence in the global market.

Management has an international component and a local one. Development strategy, product strategy, financial strategy — all these are universal. In those areas, we strive to be thorough in using international methods. In contrast to these, the local part is valuable just because it is local. For example, we had to build a mosque in our factory in Malaysia. There's no reason to deny such facets of a society.

In Japan, there is a fence named Canon that surrounds all our employees, but after work they return to being Japanese. When working in Japan you can't escape from Japanese culture and tradition. Therefore, it is more realistic to choose management principles and techniques that are based on the realities of present society than to ignore the culture. Management is a part of a society.

The Japanese have the attitude that this is, for example, the Canon duchy, or the Hitachi fief, and you can shoot them dead before they will shift alliances. I think this is a matter of Japanese culture. This is why they don't hop from one company to the next. It is the communal destiny, born of the lifetime-employment system. Employees who are part of a group sharing a common destiny gain strength at those times when they think, "Since I'm a participant in all this, I have to do something". Even if the company has a problem, even if they have to take a cut in pay, top performers don't walk. This is a characteristic of Japan.

Canon itself has never let people go. Now, in my own case, when I was young, there were two occasions when there were cuts in pay. One of those times was during the recession that followed the 1964 Tokyo Olympics — but no one quit. Because Japan possesses this awareness, it has strength against recessions. Since people do not hop from company to company for more money, quality employees do not leave. Therefore the power to recover is strong. American companies are quick to fail. This is because their quality people quit.

Lifetime employment, I think, is the spirit of Japan. You don't find it elsewhere in Asia; you won't find it in China. It is not found in American or European culture. What I would like to emphasize is that it can be developed as a source of competitiveness.

The old employment practices are fading away in many companies, and it can be said that practices which should be left behind are being abandoned. If we look back to postwar Japan, when maximizing employment was the most important issue, we had a planned economy led by the bureaucrats. Many companies were afforded protection from free markets. Moreover, there was the seniority pay system, leading to the adoption of rigid pay structures wherein there were annual increases regardless of the company's business performance. What this cost was a loss of ability to withstand the changes over time that come with financial deregulation and the opening of markets. Then it became almost unavoidable, as Japan faced more global competition, for some companies to have layoffs. I am not critical of this trend.

The drawbacks of the seniority system

Q: *But if you guarantee employment, you pamper the organization. Don't you run the risk that employees' attitudes become slack?*

M: Companies don't fail because of lifetime employment. There are some businessmen who say that it is tough to let people go at a time when the company is in trouble, but what they should have done in the first place is to manage the company so that it is healthy. This is not a problem of systems; it is a matter of too many employees — hiring more people than necessary. To have too many employees and then complain that business is bad, and then blame lifetime employment, is to confuse cause with effect. Really, if you have a small crew of talented people, you've got a terribly strong company.

Every system has its defects. Certainly, under the lifetime-employment system, employees may relax and take it easy. Education can offset that. Since its founding, management at Canon has adhered to its Three Selfs concept: self-motivation to do every job right; self-management; and self-awareness with regard to one's responsibilities. These are the qualities Canon seeks when hiring, and promotes after hiring. Therefore, for my part, I want to have a deep relationship with the employees and impart these concepts to them. Every month, I speak to a gathering of 700 or 800 managers, and once a year, while visiting our offices and factories, I get a report on the past year. And for those whom I meet, I review the past year's performance and tell them of plans for the coming year and the next five years. I have done this every year since becoming president. Nowadays it is frequently said that young people are prone to individualism and are self-centered. The men and women who join Canon have pride and come to work with us because they like the company.

Particularly because lifetime employment defines a group sharing a common destiny, everyone shares the philosophy of wanting to make the company better. As management, we should not waste resources. This means we are not going to give people work that has no future. Unless we eliminate such work and find more meaningful jobs for those people, we are courting trouble.

One more thing; the seniority system spoils people. The pay and benefits arrangements at Canon from the day the company began have always been based on meritocracy, not seniority, and are not influenced by education, age or gender. We test everyone, the method of which is disclosed to our employees, as is our method of evaluation, and anyone who passes can get promoted and make more money. Conversely, if a person doesn't take the test, his pay doesn't go up. We make it possible for people to know who took the test and who didn't. We don't pay the same to everyone; the corporate culture is one of promoting the development of employees by assuring them of a competitive environment in which there is fair recognition of their individual abilities.

Invigorating the company through fair competition

We bring out the best in a person. We motivate them through competition. We have a system that promotes people by ability and doesn't look at such matters as educational achievements. By the 1960s, we had realized sustained high-level economic growth and, since then, we have pursued egalitarianism in order to raise overall performance. In my opinion, this policy, which was intended to enable Japan to recover after the war, was not mistaken. But during that process a problem was created in that an evil egalitarianism became entrenched and we lost an awareness of competition. We suffered from an excess of what we had relied on in the past. In particular, the protected companies lost their sense of responsibility.

The most pressing issue after the end of the war was to provide relief for the unemployed. Gradually, the quality of life was raised through the workings of a de facto planned economy. In the process, we raised wages. Thus, Japan accomplished the development of a socialist national economy. Up to a certain time, that was the correct thing. It protected employment.

The companies took over responsibility for social security, which originally was the responsibility of the nation. There's nothing to be gained by saying that this was good or bad. With this behind us, now in the 21st century, can management simply destroy this history? No, we can't. Management has to be founded on the traditions of society. But we have to recognize, on the basis of an awareness of the present era, that if there is anything that will provide the strength of cohesion that will enable us survive, it is lifetime employment.

More than a business, Canon is a production floor; it is development. There are all sorts of people. I don't call it management if, for example, the focus is placed on the development teams. Management is overall strength. While always monitoring the times, I want us to create a flow in which all our people are unified.

To tell the truth, after experiencing the high growth of the 1960s, we had to convert from a philosophy of equality to one of fairness, and make it the principle on which competition was based. But we fell into recession. U.S. management style crept in. There were some who thought it was great, and leaped to adopt it. There were others who rejected it, but I was not one of them. I did not show any sign of a rejection. As an individual I had to decide on whether it was good for Japan. When making my choice, I thought that the U.S. style was not applicable in today's Japan. So we have followed a Japanese style. We may be thought of as old-fashioned, but that is how I see things.

Q: *Does Canon consider corporate culture to be an asset?*

M: Our first president, Takeshi Mitarai, who, as a doctor, had a respect for people, adopted the ideal of making a company whose employees would be able to lead happy lives. We've accepted this humanitarian belief as Canon's inheritance. We adopted, ahead of other companies, the practice of screening for tuberculosis, a five-day work week and a scheme for helping employees acquire their own home.

Differences in corporate infrastructure

What will be the best methods to raise turnover in the business climate in which companies operate today? This is the key question. In management there is an optimum set of methods for every company. The American methods that we should adopt, we adopt; we choose on the basis of whether it is good for Canon or not. If I were told to return to the U.S. and manage a company there, I would do so by replacing staff with the aim of strengthening operations. Well, when I was at the U.S. subsidiary I reduced the staffing, including managers, but it was tough to do. Even in America letting someone go is tough, not only for the employee but for the manager too. Just because it is in America doesn't mean it is a simple matter. Having had the experience of laying people off in the U.S., I am extremely careful not to create a situation where I would have to do so again.

Q: *Will a change in Japan's industrial structure take place?*

M: If this is taken as a national issue, that is the right question. I'm not totally rejecting greater mobility of workers, but I think it has to be promoted as national policy, as in America. In any case, you can't have management that ignores a country's broad social environment. For example, the total number of companies in the United States is nearly four times that in Japan, so there are many employment opportunities. Furthermore, since pay levels for specific occupations, or in specific regions, are known, it is easy to change jobs. The tax system and other arrangements favor the formation of venture companies and there is a steady stream of new companies being created; meaning more jobs.

On the premise that the social infrastructure is in place in this manner, I wouldn't say that I am opposed to greater worker mobility. There would be many good aspects. In Japan, we have to create more companies and make the environment conducive to aggressive investment in plant and equipment by small and medium-scale businesses. We probably have to take in more direct investment from overseas.

Q: *What of the matter that conditions are not yet in place in Japan for mobility of labor?*

M: That's right. That's why we can judge that at the present time there is a great advantage in the lifetime-employment system. Businesses exist within a country, not the reverse. It is nonsense to make a simple comparison of American and Japanese employment practices — it amounts to nothing less than comparing apples with oranges.

But we are all anxiously awaiting a conversion of Japan's industrial structure. We hear the opinion that all the redundant personnel that companies are carrying should be reduced and labor mobility should be promoted.

There will be some who will manage to swim away once they have been pushed overboard, but about half of those let go will drown. Why, we have some people at Canon that simply couldn't work for any other company. If a large number of companies abdicated their responsibilities as employers, the unemployment rate would surge. It is likely that crime would increase as a result. In order to prevent that, it is necessary to be ready for a rise in social security costs. What policies should we pursue as a nation? This is a political decision.

Without improving the infrastructure by increasing the number of newly created jobs, improving the unemployment insurance system and expanding vocational training, we will not be able to achieve greater mobility. What we have to do in Japan first is to improve the infrastructure.

Ideally, when conditions are right, a company will adopt lifetime employment. When we have affluent companies at the time when the infrastructure for labor mobility has been improved, and workers can move, all of them in those companies will continue to work there because they prefer it — that is the kind of company I want Canon to be.

Q: *Isn't it difficult to achieve profit growth while retaining the lifetime-employment system in the present economic environment?*

M: Japan must preserve its industry. We have to make inexpensive products, using new systems and new technology, in order to accomplish this. If labor costs rise despite whatever is done, manufacturers must continue to transform themselves into higher value-added industries. One way to achieve this is through innovation. Another way is to use R&D activities as a driving force for transformation of the company. The company then has to be in good financial shape in order to continue investing in R&D. That is why I have had the goal, since becoming CEO, of making high profits.

To pay profits to the shareholders, to improve the livelihood of employees, to contribute to society, and to have the leeway to invest in order to make the company grow — these are the four conditions management must satisfy. Unless these conditions are met, the company is of no value. That is why profits are most important of all. They make it possible to have the strength to create new businesses; to protect the lifetime-employment system; and to manage the effects of fluctuations in the exchange rate.

Q: *Canon's performance at this time is good. But what do you do if it becomes necessary to make a drastic cut in labor costs?*

M: Not by reducing staff; first of all we cut salaries. Then there is work sharing. I will take a cut in my own pay if conditions demand it. I'll continue the fight even if it is cut to zero. By this means the cohesiveness of the company overall becomes stronger, and recovery is accelerated. If conditions grow ever worse, then it will become necessary to reduce the number of employees; but when that happens I will probably no longer be in the company. I work every day at ensuring that that won't happen.

American-style methods for managing reform

Q: *Why is it that you have adopted such American-style methods as cash-flow management, consolidated management, and dropping unprofitable business lines?*

M: A management approach has to be effective as a means of achieving a profit by investing capital. Pursuing sales growth without regard to profits means obtaining all the working capital through borrowing. Even at Canon, the business division-based system that was a success in the 1980s was carried to extremes and each division became too large. So we then adopted a system of evaluating the performance of each division on a consolidated basis, and emphasized cash-flow management in order to make investments without relying on borrowing. Although we lost some ¥30 billion in sales when we dropped out of the personal computer business, a loss of more than 10 billion was also eliminated from the bottom line. We spared nothing in rationalizing, from development to production to marketing, and improved our financial position.

Q: *You've emphasized that the American system of independent directors and executive officers is not needed at Canon. What is your reason for saying this?*

M: At many Japanese companies, the board and the executives are one and the same. This is because Japanese officials both make and enforce laws. When an executive committee meeting is held, management policy is determined from the viewpoint of a legislator. Then, on the ground, they implement the decision.

It takes two to three decades to become a director in a Japanese company. During that period, there is a continuous top-to-bottom check of the person's character and ability. The Japanese method is safer than that of the United States, where managers are brought in from outside. If you were to base your argument on the frequency of crimes committed by executives, there is no need in Japan to make a new executive committee. I think this would hamper more than help.

Having said that, any system will have its defects. There are defects in the Japanese systems. Because the executives are like an "old-boys club", each executive is reluctant to offend the others. Sure, the check functions work in the American system. But in Japan we set up the system of statutory auditors to perform the check function in the manner of European or American companies. We don't have boards. I think the auditor system is better. The reason for this is that the statutory auditor is in the company every day, watching the executives work. In contrast to this, the outside directors come to the company only once a quarter. I serve as an outside director at a U.S. company, but I don't understand the nitty-gritty details of the business. When something is to be decided, I give my opinion from an objective viewpoint but I don't offer my opinion about specific events in the company. The Americans are the same way. Thus, the outside-director system has its limits. By legally strengthening the position and function of the statutory auditor, we can have an improved regulatory function in Japan.

Now there are some who say that it is a good idea to bring in a president from outside; that in this way something new in the corporate culture can be created; but I think this is wrong. I heard Jack Welch say that in the hundred years of GE's history there has not been one president brought in from outside and that it would stay like this. Doesn't bringing in a president from outside indicate a failure to develop a next-generation CEO? We have plenty of talented people at Canon. Naturally, we will pick successors from among them.

THE COMMON-DESTINY PARADIGM

Mitarai stresses the point that this system is being maintained in order to protect the employees' awareness of sharing a common destiny. His thinking is that a company whose employees possess this awareness has outstanding power to bounce back when facing a threat.

This is not necessarily an offbeat way of thinking. The majority of postwar Japanese companies grew on the strength of this concept. It was the prolonged downturn of the 1990s that forced a number of companies, which could not bear the burden of personnel costs, to change direction. In this regard, there has been a complete change of scenery. When a majority of employees were hired under the mutual assumption of a lifetime commitment, there is, quite naturally, anxiety regarding the threat to morale when such a change of direction is undertaken, and the risk is great. A sense of a common destiny is still strong within Canon, and Mitarai believes the company is better off shoring it up than scrapping it. That is his considered judgment. And this is not a matter of emotion overriding logic.

THE FOUNTAINHEAD OF CORPORATE CULTURE — PHILOSOPHIES OF THE FIRST PRESIDENT

Neo-paternalism: Bonding by a common destiny

At Canon, this awareness of belonging to a group sharing a common destiny may be expressed in the term "neo-paternalism" advocated by Takeshi Mitarai, the company's first president. The 60th-anniversary issue of *Canon Life*, the company's inhouse magazine, carries a quote from him that expounds on this idea: "Not the kind of paternalism that smells of feudalism, where everything is decided at the top My brand of neo-paternalism is where we come together and know each other, in sorrow and in joy." This is the Canon corporate philosophy in which the workforce is seen as a quasi-family.

In August 1937, when the firm was made into a joint-stock company in the precision-optics industry it had about 60 employees and was hard pressed to meet its payroll obligations. But a club was formed. In 1946, it held a sports event. Then in the following year there was a party held for employees and their families at which awards were given to those employees who had given many years of service to the company. In 1963 an award, the Family Peace Prize, was established for all employees who had a five-year record of not being late and not taking sick leave. The recipients were also invited to an evening of Kabuki or some other theatrical entertainment.

Representative of the club's activities were the birthday parties, held monthly from 1953 to 1964, when all employees having a birthday in that month were invited to bring their families to the company to celebrate their birthday and good health, with president Mitarai and other officers of the company as hosts. There would be a cake-cutting ceremony by the president together with a representative of the employees, and food, soft drinks and beer were provided to all those attending. As part of the celebrations, all present would sing and dance to "The Canon Song". The company song, with lyrics by Yaso Saijo and music by Masao Koga, two

Canon's first president, Takeshi Mitarai (far right), cuts a cake in this 1958 photo taken at one of the company's birthday parties for employees and families, which were held monthly between 1953 and 1964

prominent popular musicians of the day, had been created in 1952, in connection with the 15th anniversary of the founding of the company. In 1961, all employees of the company were given a recording of "The Birthday Song", composed by the well-known Hachiro Sato and Ryoichi Hattori, and sung by the Dark Ducks, a popular vocal group.

The Canon Song extols the first president's neo-paternalism. There was at times a bit of hostility toward the song.

The Canon Song

1. *Where the Tama River flows*
    A ring of flowers blooms —
    Canon, finest flower
    Of all the flowers that bloom.

Continued

The Canon Song—cont'd

Where the Tama rapids roar
There the youthful Ayu (sweetfish) dance —
We who are so young
Dance with high energy.
We who are so young
Dance with high energy.

2. *In the cool shade of trees*
   My young wife strikes a pose
   My winning children smile
   Smiles of pure delight.

   Click! My Canon's cunning lens
   Lets no shadow fall on them
   It will not allow
   Any darkness where they walk.
   It will not allow
   Any darkness where they walk.

3. *Oh, the Canon Ondo*
   Truly International,
   How beautifully all move,
   How beautifully all move.
   Hands shaping graceful curves

   Making their land grow,
   Growing as their nation grows,
   A whirlpool of pride.
   Growing as their nation grows,
   A whirlpool of pride.

Rendered by Alfred H. Marks

One year, when the employees had gathered to celebrate the Buddhist *obon* festival — a celebration that includes dancing in a circle — there was a complaint from some that they didn't come to the company to dance. But Takeshi Mitarai declared that everyone must dance. While elements of this thinking may now seem a little outdated, when some think of the incident today they can smile.

Mitarai's neo-paternalism also incorporated the idea that health comes first, which is part of the company motto. In 1967, Canon adopted the five-day work week — the first Japanese company to do so. Takeshi Mitarai explained why the company did this in an interview in 1978 on the principle that a shorter work week resulted in a healthier and more productive staff: "Rather than work Monday to Saturday, working Monday to Friday gives you time to spend with the family, time to rest and have some energy stored up when starting work on Monday."

In another step to promote health, Takeshi Mitarai devised a special exercise routine in 1967, an idea found in many Japanese companies. These calisthenics, designed to foster the health of employees, to strengthen their bodies, to prevent injuries and to help refresh them when tired, were taught in the workplace. It might be said that, in this context, the relationship between Takeshi Mitarai — the obstetrician — and the employees was as much that of a physician and his patients as that of an executive and workers.

Labor–management consultation

The effects of Mitarai's neo-paternalism were also evident in the company's relations with the union. Canon employees formed a company union in July 1946, at a time when labor was very active, in the aftermath of the war and early days of reconstruction. But they didn't call it a labor union; they called it an employees' union. Behind the nomenclature was the sense of sharing a destiny, a sense reinforced by the text of the founding declaration, which included the following words: "Workers must band together to protect profits, but there is no meaning to the union's surviving when the company fails. The pursuit of profit is a common objective of workers and the employer, and the issue of allocation of profits follows from that."

The pay system adopted after the union was formed was, and remains, an incentive-based system. Incentives are paid during the month, and since wages are paid at the end of the month, the system in effect creates two pay days a month.

A collective-bargaining agreement was signed in August 1946, and consultative meetings are still held, in the form of labor–management conferences. The following year saw the inception of arrangements for annual pay raises and lump-sum retirement bonuses.

The "Canon three-way theory" for splitting profits was adopted in July 1950. This calls for dividing profits three ways; between the company, the stockholders, and the employees. The share given to employees was based on profit expectations, and was paid as twice-yearly bonuses. If actual profits at the end of the fiscal year exceeded the anticipated amount, one-third of the difference was paid to employees. In time, this method of calculating was reviewed and, in 1964, was dropped.

Paternalism and meritocracy

Neo-paternalism and an awareness of having a common destiny are two major roots of the Canon corporate culture. But there is a third factor — meritocracy — that has to be added to the mix.

For ordinary employees at Canon, October is showdown month. The last week in every October is "promotion exam" time. Fail the test, and the opportunity to reach management level is lost. This system was adopted by Takeshi Mitarai in 1963, together with a work performance assessment known as the "ability-qualification system." In these is embodied Canon's tradition of meritocracy.

High school graduates sit for their first exam eight years after joining the company. College graduates sit for the exam after four years, and for employees joining out of graduate school the exam comes after two years. Alternatively, employees have to take the exam in the first October after passing their 25th birthday. No distinction is made between men and women. The company requires employees to take the exam at least twice. The first part of the test determines whether a person can be promoted to a specialist grade. The next part determines whether an employee can get promoted to "assistant to manager" grade or, in the case of technical personnel, "assistant engineer" grade. There would be a pay differential of about 20% between two 30-year-old employees of whom one has reached the highest pre-managerial level by passing all tests the first time, and the other who has passed no tests at all.

The first part of the exam comprises multiple-choice questions. The second, in essay form, tests general knowledge and work-related knowledge. Those who pass both parts sit for the third part, an interview (specialist-grade personnel are exempt from this requirement). Scoring is impartial. On the written parts of the exam, numbers rather than names are used to identify the employees and to prevent possible discretionary judgment by scorers. The essays are checked by five people, the highest and lowest scores are eliminated, and an average is taken of the remaining three.

"This is all done purely on merit," Fujio Mitarai says. "There's no discrimination by gender, age, or educational accomplishments. This really gives Canon energy."

In 1943, the year after he become the company's first president, Takeshi Mitarai eliminated the practice of paying workers a daily wage and started paying by the month. At that time, ordinary companies had a dual system that divided those who worked for them into employees and factory workers. Convention had the former enter by the front door, and the latter by the back door. It was normal for workers to be paid by the work they accomplished, for which reason no workers would share their expertise with others. They were like hired hands, scrambling to finish one product and moving on to another. It occurred to Mitarai that he would rather have everyone work together to help surmount the problems of wartime. So he abolished the worker class, making everyone a company employee and paying everyone by the month. "If we pay people like day laborers, they are not going to be able to have a stable livelihood. If they get sick, they lose their way of gaining income," he reasoned. "Paying by the month is a way of respecting employees as people, and if they are serious about their work, it stabilizes their livelihood."

Meritocracy, whereby all employees are treated fairly, has been a Canon tradition since that time. The current president Mitarai says on the subject: "Right now, today, all of this seems quite ordinary but, at the time, replacing a system based on education with one based on merit was extremely novel. What happened is that many technical workers and engineers of substantial ability came to Canon looking for work. All this was a result of Takeshi Mitarai's idealism. We had the workforce we needed, and they injected plenty of energy into the company."

High pay for high efficiency

During the postwar era of sustained growth, Canon came to be known as a company that paid high salaries for high efficiency. In 1957, at the crest of what was known as the "Jimmu boom" (after a mythological emperor), popular writer Soichi Ohya wrote about Canon in a series for the *Weekly Asahi* magazine. After visiting the company, he wrote: "With the motto of doing away with cliques and linking high pay with high ability, carrying out the policy of a three-way sharing of profits — between the suppliers of capital, the managers of the company and the employees — has meant there is no strife at Canon. I am told that an engineer can earn as much as ¥100,000 a month." The average pay when Ohya visited the company was ¥30,160. At the time, the nationwide average for manufacturing was ¥17,500.

The *Weekly Asahi* returned to cover Canon in 1962. This time, it was to write up Takeshi Mitarai's advocacy of punctuality. "Work starts at 8 in the morning and ends at 4:45 in the afternoon. The lunch break is 45 minutes long and no provision is made for any other rest periods. 'The taxi fares I have to pay out in order to clock in at 8 are a shame. Punch in after 8 and it is treated as if you are taking a holiday. The executives also show up at 8,' says a woman employee, age 25."

Takeshi Mitarai was very strict about punctuality and if a visitor were late for an appointment, Mitarai would not see him, no matter how important the visitor. Mitarai would always start conferences on time, even if not all participants were in attendance. In 1963, the company also adopted a system of compensation and promotions that was tied to ability, known as the ability-qualification system. The system came to symbolize Canon's meritocracy, and became a standard at Canon much earlier than at many other Japanese companies. With a few small modifications, this meritocratic system remains intact today.

RENAISSANCE OF THE CORPORATE CULTURE

Repairing the meritocracy: Reforming personnel and pay systems

About the time when Fujio Mitarai returned from the U.S. in 1989, hairline cracks were developing in Canon's corporate culture and, in particular, in deeper parts of the meritocracy. The meritocratic system, the cornerstone of the personnel and pay systems, was showing signs of institutional fatigue. Years of experience (generally a function of age) had come to be a central criterion for measuring ability to perform on the job. Rather than set remuneration fairly and equally according to the employee's level of responsibility and accomplishments, it rewarded according to age. The pay system, in effect, had acquired the nature of a seniority system.

It had become obvious that one of the drawbacks that had accompanied the introduction of the various business divisions was that the evaluation of personnel was being made solely on the basis of conditions in the relevant department or section. This meant losing a uniform standard. To remedy this, in 1993, a manual was prepared, giving detailed methodology for evaluation of managers at department head level and above, but this alone was not enough.

"The company had continued to adhere to the policy of bringing out the individuality and the best of everyone through fair competition," says Mitarai. He was shocked to find signs of the crumbling of Canon's meritocracy. So, while setting about getting the company out of unprofitable businesses and reforming production, he took the opportunity to introduce measures designed to protect the merit-based system around which the company was built.

In February 2000, Mitarai instructed the head of human resources, Keijiro Yamazaki, to review the pay system and, if possible, to implement changes with effect from April that year. Behind this decision lay progress in reforming the production system and early signs that the company's financial position was improving.

There were three broad objectives in view here: to get rid of automatic annual pay raises; to ensure fairness and equality; and to introduce a scheme that would be globally applicable. At the time, however, annual pay negotiations with the union had already begun and it seemed impossible to accomplish the changes in the time available. Yamazaki explained the situation to Mitarai, who agreed to postpone the implementation of new arrangements until April 2001. Even then, time was short. In some companies it takes two or three years to shake up personnel and pay systems. Yamazaki started work at once.

Yamazaki organized a team inside the Human Resources department in April 2000. He called it his JK Project Team — "J" was for *jinji* ("personnel") and K was for *kakushin* ("reform") — and began searching for companies which had pay schemes that satisfied all of Mitarai's conditions. Believing that relying on inhouse resources alone would not be sufficient to meet Mitarai's requirements, Yamazaki spoke to outside experts and began to assemble the framework for change.

The JK Project Team — consisting of four people, including Yamazaki, from the Canon parent company, and two people from the domestic sales subsidiary, Canon Sales — was the core group for promoting the reform movement in personnel affairs.

The team set out to identify the basic concept for the new system, and the rationale that would support it. Among the problems it faced was the fact that the pay system had become transformed into a seniority-based system. The fundamental rationale for this equated years of experience with improved ability to work, which therefore led to improved performance. But there was no reason to expect that two people with the same years of experience would have the same capabilities.

Another problem was that even when the system was operating in strict adherence to its tenets, suitable positions were not always available to enable those with ability to make full use of it. "As long as the workforce was increasing while the company grew, the problems of a de facto seniority system tended to be overlooked as there were opportunities for everyone. But once the company's global staff level stabilized at about 20,000, distortions appeared," recalls senior managing director Yukio Yamashita, who heads the Human Resources Management & Organization Headquarters.

Fixing the ability-qualification system

How could Canon balance the work that an employee was doing with the pay provided for that work? The JK Project Team began searching for a metric that would enable Canon to maintain its traditions of meritocracy and respect for the individual, even though times had changed. The search led from a standard based on the individual to one based on the work.

Payment according to the job assigned is the general practice in the United States, where the accounting department says it should be a certain level, and the personnel department says it should be a certain level, and the amount is determined more or less automatically. There, the job description is defined in great detail. There is no relationship at all to experience or age in most cases in the U.S. model. While this was a scheme appropriate for those who would abandon the seniority system, any attempt to introduce such a system in one fell swoop at a company where the ability-qualification system had become entrenched, would undoubtedly cause great confusion. To define in detailed terms what each specific job entailed threatened the flexibility of the company to cope with change in the kind of business it is engaged in. What rescued Yamashita from this problem was the concept of wage range by job classification.

Here, "range" refers to the role associated with the job. It combines the flexible element of job responsibility and is not simply a matter of a detailed statement of a rigid assignment, as in the U.S. For example, in the case of a personnel department manager, the work requirements are management of hiring, assignment and promotion. As the job responsibility may change from year to year, this is determined by a meeting with the manager's superior.

Yamazaki and his team adopted a five-grade scheme, from M1 to M5, for managerial-level personnel. M1 was for Senior Staff Engineer or Senior Staff, and M2 to M5 were, respectively, for manager (*kacho*, department chief), general manager (*bucho*, division chief), senior general manager (*shocho*) and, at the top, group executive (*honbucho*).

Within each grade, the pay had a specific range. A range was called a "mission band". For each band, the lowest level was specified as the base, and additions were to be made according to evaluations. Within a band, pay for a given individual would rise or fall according to the evaluation. The current system too had a range similar to these bands. The wage range by job classification arrangement falls somewhere between job-based pay and the ability-qualification system. Evaluation for levels above the "mission" base was done by judging results and the person. In judging whether the employee produced results, the means of measurement is important. If the means of measurement doesn't match the realities of the work performed, the worker will lose motivation and there is a danger that the competitiveness of the organization will suffer. Recognizing this, the project team added "degree of fulfillment of mission", "extent of execution of work" and "behavior standard" to the existing management-by-objectives approach. Within the "mission", items for the degree of stress the job entailed and the importance of the job were provided. Further, "extent of execution

Organization and hierarchy of managerial-level positions, before and after reform

OLD CLASSIFICATION		NEW CLASSIFICATION	
Sanji 1			
Sanji 2		M5	Group executive (Honbucho)
Assistant Sanji 1		M4	Senior general manager (Shocho)
Assistant Sanji 2		M3	General manager (Bucho, division chief)
Shuji 1	Engineer 1	M2	Manager (Kacho, department chief)
Shuji 2	Engineer 2	M1	Senior staff engineer (for technical staff) or senior staff (for administrative staff; Sennin shukan); also project manager (Ekisupato shoku)

(Above: managerial level; below: general employees)

OLD CLASSIFICATION		NEW CLASSIFICATION	
Shuji assistant 1	Engineer assistant 1	J4	Assistant manager (Kacho-dairi)
Shuji assistant 2	Engineer assistant 2	J3	Employees are promoted to J3 upon passing their second promotion test
Specialist Grade 1		J2	Employees are promoted to J2 upon passing their first promotion test
Specialist Grade 2		J1	For new recruits who have graduated from a four-year university course
D Grade		E	For new recruits who have graduated from high school, junior college, or professional school
C Grade			
B Grade			
A Grade			
S Grade			

of work" evaluates the process whereby tasks were accomplished. Behavior standard measures whether the person is the right one for the job, and is based on "Canon Behavioral Standard", "Fairness and Equality", "Self-Improvement" and "Attitudes towards Mission". But often in that process low-level objectives are adopted, so that they can be easily accomplished. The three measurement aspects adopted at Canon were intended to offset the defects inherent in management by objectives.

Adopting a system with a range of wages according to job classification meant that values had to be set for all sorts of jobs, and "missions" had to be classified. So Yamazaki asked a consulting company to evaluate 5,600 jobs in the Canon group, both in Japan and overseas. He and his project team undertook detailed planning for the pay system and, through their efforts, the details of the new system had been worked out by September 2000.

Rapid shift to the new system

After securing Mitarai's approval for the new system in October, Yamazaki held briefing and training sessions for managers during November and December. In April 2001, just one year after the project team had been formed, and right on schedule, the system kicked in for all managers at Canon headquarters and Canon Sales. "To the extent that we added a Canon flavoring to the new system, I guess you could say that it was not that revolutionary," says Yamazaki. Nevertheless, it certainly was exceptional among Japanese companies to implement a change such as this in just one year.

Previously, the monthly pay of managers had consisted of several components; the base pay, which was determined on the basis of both the ability and the age of the employee; and several allowances, such as a position allowance, a family allowance and a subsidy for meals. Bonuses were a multiple of the monthly base pay, and generally were the same across the board. The variable amount, determined by an evaluation of the individual manager's performance, was a small percentage of the whole. The new system introduced a base pay component, determined by the "mission", and an individual evaluation component. Bonuses were calculated by adding to the monthly pay an amount based on the company's business performance.

A complete removal of the allowances — particularly the family allowance — posed a real headache. This was because the allowances were closely associated with neo-paternalism, that basic component of the company's culture. While there was no direct relationship between neo-paternalism and the family allowance, the allowance had come to be taken for granted and there were concerns that this new system would be seen by employees as if it were a complete abandonment of neo-paternalism.

Were allowances unrelated to the results of work to be retained, namely to the performance of a unit of the company, this would undermine the basis of the personnel and pay system reforms. Mitarai's conviction on this point was of some influence, and all allowances were ended. To ensure that this did not damage the sense of a shared destiny at Canon, the company held many meetings and ran many training programs to explain the changes to employees. "We've evolved from what has existed up to now," says Yamazaki.

It was planned to have all Canon group companies in Japan adopt the new system from April 2002. When the system was expanded to incorporate non-managerial personnel, annual raises would end.

Mitarai was pleased with the new system. "We are going to adopt a merit-based pay system that will be valid even for Canon group companies outside of Japan," he said. "In the future, we may have Europeans transfer to the U.S. or to Asia. I want to see a system that permits free movement everywhere."

In order to ease the shock of the new system, it was ruled that, in principle, the monthly base pay portions would not be reduced from existing levels. Nevertheless, because the new system was applicable to bonuses without any such modification, a considerable difference in cash terms resulted.

Conceptual diagram of the old and new pay systems (managerial level)

OLD SYSTEM

Monthly pay	Base pay (Determined by abilities and age) Position allowance, Family allowance, Subsidy for meals
Bonus	Base pay × no. of months (No. of months same for all employees) Individual performance

NEW SYSTEM

Monthly pay	Individual performance Monthly base pay (Determined by mission)	
Bonus	Base bonus (Determined by mission)	
	Performance-based bonus	Individual performance
		Company performance

As the new evaluation system becomes better established and pay differentials develop for people who have the same mission, then the changes that have been made will become much more evident. There will likely be cases where people who entered the company at the same time have different mission grades, and instances when someone who entered earlier than another person has a lower grade than the other. A transfer may result in a person's working for a boss who has the same grade, or may put an employee to work under a boss of a lower grade. A transfer will not influence the pay given for the employee's grade, but the bonus will be subject to change, as it will become what has been determined for the new unit. When an employee's job changes, the pay generally will rise, or will fall. It will not change according to years of service. In the old days when pay was job-based, it went up from year to year and never declined. Hereafter, the strict meritocracy at Canon is going to become built into the company more and more.

Concurrent with the introduction of the new personnel and pay systems, a lowering of the average age of managers was encouraged. Under the old system, employees could become a manager (department chief) at age 35; the new system lowered the promotion age to 32. General managers (division heads) could now be appointed at 35, as opposed to 40 in the past. Before the reforms, the spread between the minimum and maximum pay an employee aged 35 could receive was 1.4 times; this rose to 1.8 times after the changes. For someone aged 40, the difference rose from 1.6 times to double.

Motivating with incentives

Rewarding those employees who realize the full extent of their abilities is vital if meritocracy is to be thoroughly established. Awarding everybody the same, regardless of performance, acts as a strong disincentive to those who produce results. Bonuses and promotions are only part of the company's system for ensuring that those who produce significant results are properly rewarded.

It has always been part of the Canon tradition to recognize outstanding contributions from its employees. For example, in 1946, the company began to give awards for employees' inventions. Though modified somewhat over the years, this arrangement is still in place today and works in the following way.

Whenever employees submit a patent application or register an invention, they are paid a sum of up to ¥10,000. A patent-screening committee, chaired by the executive in charge of the Corporate Intellectual Property & Legal Headquarters, evaluates each submission on a seven-point scale. Doing it this way helps ensure objectivity and transparency, and the committee also determines what sorts of inventions qualify and decides on the level or amount of the award. Payment of the top two awards requires approval by the Executive Committee.

There is also the President's Award, which is given to the group or individual that devises a patented invention that makes a significant contribution to the performance of the company. While the amounts are not great, the awards serve to recognize achievement and ensure that such contributions are known widely within the company.

The company has long had a policy of celebrating milestone events by making modest cash awards to employees. In 1954, for example, when a loan of US$500,000 was repaid to the British trading firm Jardine Matheson in just three years, all employees were given a small cash payment in celebration.

At the end of 1996, when the company's recurring profit passed the ¥100 billion mark, everyone received a small gift. "Early that year, we informed our employees that it was essential that we achieve the level of ¥100 billion in profits," Mitarai says. "When we succeeded in doing it that very year, we gave everyone a bonus." All employees, even those who had been working for Canon for only a matter of months, received ¥70,000 each. To mark the company's 60th anniversary in 1997, all employees were given ¥120,000. This is very much Mitarai's style.

Also, in December 2000, every employee was given ¥150,000 to commemorate the realization of goals set in the Excellent

Global Corporation Plan and the start of a new millennium. "We wanted to celebrate having become a sustainable-profit company in the five years up to that time, and I sent a personal letter to all employees explaining how I felt about their efforts towards that end," says Mitarai. The letter also reinforced the importance of cash-flow management and, by extension, of focusing on profit. On Christmas Eve, two bottles of wine arrived at the home of every employee, in celebration of the listing of Canon's shares on the New York Stock Exchange. Parcel-delivery companies were kept busy delivering some 40,000 bottles.

When the bonuses are paid every year, in summer and in winter, as is Japanese custom, Mitarai makes a point of shaking the hand of every employee of general manager or higher level — that's 800 or so handshakes — giving them their bonus envelopes and telling them how he appreciates their efforts, often with the words *gokuro sama* ("good job"). "My hands get swollen," he admits. "But this is the way things are done in Japan and it's absolutely essential."

A word about the Excellent Global Corporation Plan. It was launched in 1996 as a five-year management initiative with a range of concrete targets. When this concluded in 2000, with the meeting of all targets, the company then launched Phase II in 2001. This second plan is also a five-year program that calls for the realization of additional objectives to be achieved by 2005 (including becoming No. 1 in all major areas of business, along with sales and profit targets). Mitarai uses the expression "a truly excellent global corporation" to convey what would commonly be referred to as a blue-chip company. His efforts as CEO have been aimed at transforming Canon into a truly excellent global corporation.

One example of the transformation of Canon was the new system that gave production-floor employees a reinvigorated attitude: the "Master Craftsman" system for technical staff charged with metalworking and other processes, and the "Meister" system for the employees in charge of assembly work.

The Master Craftsman appellation was used for workers who polish lenses, apply coatings, install wiring, and do other work aside from actual assembly. They are evaluated for their technical skill according to a three-level grading system (A, B and C). A technician or engineer who displays the highest levels of knowledge and ability will be given the top rating of A. At Canon's factories there is a tradition of putting in applications for recognition of such technical proficiency on behalf of employees to related public institutions.

In addition to receiving an honorarium of ¥500,000, the engineer in question is given the responsibility to train his successors. Perhaps two successors are selected, and they must learn from the Master Craftsman over a period of two years. The Master Craftsman is given a budget of up to ¥1 million to buy materials or equipment needed to transfer his expertise and skills to the others. Master Craftsmen also benefit from an extension of their post-retirement contract work beyond the mandatory retirement age of 60. While employees in general are limited to three years of such employment, a Master Craftsman is entitled to five years. The age of the Master Craftsmen averages 54 years, so they must pass on what they have learned within a decade or so before they retire.

The Meister system covers employees who are in charge of the assembly of copiers or cameras. Typically, awards are made to those workers with multiple skills — who see to it that the assembly of these products is accomplished swiftly, who provide oversight of vendors, who redesign jigs in the shop and who are in charge of inspecting products.

Unlike the Master Craftsman system, the Meister system encompasses employees at all Canon group companies, domestic and overseas. Managers are not eligible. In this system, rather than look for a few outstanding individuals, the basic idea is to bring as many persons as possible into the system. In 2001, those who were designated in the system were, on average, 36 years old. Canon is considering linking acknowledgement under the Meister System with levels of pay.

The switchover to the cell system of production was the background against which the Meister system was adopted.

As mentioned earlier, the cell system is well fitted to producing small lots of a large variety of products, contributing to improvements in a company's finances while, at the same time, reducing inventory. But in order to take this up a notch, it is important to develop multi-skilled workers. Improving productivity through the cell system is the underlying objective in promoting competition among production workers. The transition to the cell system is being advanced at Canon's overseas operations as well as in Japan, and it is intended to increase the number of multi-skilled workers on a global basis.

Forging employees

Strengthening and invigorating employees — educating and training the company's human resources — is another integral part of corporate culture at Canon. The earliest mention of training in the corporate history comes in 1953, with a reference to the training of new employees. Training on a significant scale, however, began only after a technical training center was opened in about 1959, and was primarily for managers and engineers. The Human Resources Development Center, now a part of the Human Resources Management & Organization Headquarters, a special-skills training department, and an R&D technology section are now the vehicles for providing training for the R&D wing of the company.

Group training is done in eight subject areas or specialized subjects. Training has either a domestic or international orientation, and technical or engineering training in particular has become well developed. From a menu of more than 80 items on offer, employees can choose from courses related to quality control, materials technology, automation technology and business management. All of these, though, are far outnumbered by offerings in the software area.

These can be supplemented by distance-learning ventures into management, foreign languages, and other more specialized subjects using Canon's intranet. The ability to adapt to changing circumstances is as evident in human-resources development as elsewhere in the Canon organization. When, for instance, consultants were brought in to provide training for implementing production-floor reforms, employees were selected from among those had been trained and were assigned the task of teaching others in the company. The Master Craftsman and Meister systems were introduced not just to stimulate employees, but also as a training mechanism. Training was also incorporated into the KI activities that were used to promote development reforms.

"Lifetime employment has a defect in that an employee who gets too comfy under that system will lose his edge," Mitarai says. "The company's education programs are a means to offset that danger." Canon expects to make further improvements in its training programs. Getting out of unprofitable, unpromising lines may well take place again in the future. At such times, maximum use of the training system will be made to support re-assignments within the company — that's Canon's style.

Transmitting the vision

Mitarai is effusive about the philosophy underlying the company's activities. "I love the idealism of our first president. I think it is my mandate to transmit that idealism to this company," he says. He has continued to use every possible occasion — meeting with employees, visiting production sites or at other times — to convey the Canon culture that is based on a shared destiny and on meritocracy.

"Renaissance. I want to provoke a renaissance of the Three Selfs: self-motivation, self-management, and self-awareness," Mitarai says. Anyone who comes to inquire about a job with Canon gets briefed on the Three Selfs.

"Self-motivation means being proactive and aggressive with regard to whatever the task at hand is. This is a far cry from the position where an employee cannot do anything without receiving orders from his boss. Self-management means maintaining firm discipline over oneself. If a promise is made, it must be kept. If something must be done, check on it without having to be told to do so. Follow the rules."

He also expounds on the subject of self-awareness: "One must always bear in mind one's position, one's mission, and the prevailing conditions ... [employees] must know what their boss and those around them expect and must think back on how work is going and what action is being taken. Then you must have the attitude of being prepared to adjust your own course."

Of course Canon is not alone in having a vision of what a world-class company should be and what it expects of its employees. Johnson and Johnson, for example, spells this out in its Our Credo document (see next page).

A trait that is shared by a vast number of the world's leading companies is a clear idea of the role they should play in business and in society at large. Mitarai is unequivocal on this point. "What is a company? It must assure a stable livelihood for the employees, earn profits for the stockholders, contribute to society, and invest for the future. Unless these are reasonably satisfied, the company can't continue to exist."

The third president, Ryuzaburo Kaku, carried founding president Takeshi Mitarai's views on respect for individuals and sharing in a common destiny further, by enunciating the concept of *kyosei*, which Canon commonly defines as "living and working together for the common good". A more detailed definition would be: "All people, regardless of race, religion or culture, harmoniously living and working together into the future." Keizo Yamaji, who succeeded Kaku as president, then took this a step further to embrace environment-related issues.

Now, Mitarai, in his turn, is expanding this to a global scale. "Today there are many imbalances that hamper *kyosei*: trade imbalances, income imbalances (differentials between industrialized and developing countries), and world environment imbalances (such as the imbalance between development and environmental protection). Canon will proactively strive to eliminate these imbalances, by utilizing its accomplishments in *kyosei*. The truly global company, of course, develops relationships with its customers and its community as a

Johnson and Johnson: Our Credo

We believe our first responsibility is to the doctors,
nurses and patients, to mothers and fathers and all others
who use our products and services.
In meeting their needs everything we do must be of high quality.
We must constantly strive to reduce our costs
in order to maintain reasonable prices.
Customers' orders must be serviced promptly and accurately.
Our suppliers and distributors must have an opportunity
to make a fair profit.

We are responsible to our employees,
the men and women who work with us through the world.
Everyone must be considered as an individual.
We must respect their dignity and recognize their merit.
They must have a sense of security in their jobs.
Compensation must be fair and adequate,
and working conditions clean, orderly and safe.
We must be mindful of ways to help our employees fulfill
their family responsibilities.
Employees must feel free to make suggestions and complaints.
There must be equal opportunity for employment, development
and advancement for those qualified.
We must provide competent management,
and their actions must be just and ethical.

We are responsible to the communities in which we live and work
and to the world community as well.
We must be good citizens — support good works and charities
and bear our fair share of taxes.
We must encourage civic improvements and better health
and education. We must maintain in good order
the property we are privileged to use,
protecting the environment and natural resources.

Our final responsibility is to our stockholders.
Business must make a sound profit.
We must experiment with new ideas.
Research must be carried on, innovative programs developed
and mistakes paid for.
New equipment must be purchased, new facilities provided
and new products launched.
Reserves must be created to provide for adverse times.
When we operate according to these principles,
the stockholders should realize a fair return.

matter of course, but we have to expect that it will also do so with regard to the country and region, and nature, accepting social responsibility in the process." Mitarai has made *kyosei* the core corporate philosophy of Canon as a global company.

Professor Ikujiro Nonaka, of Hitotsubashi University, has commented on this philosophy, pointing out that "the relativistic view that holds that all that is important is to whip the other guy in competition doesn't assign much value to the company. It is precisely the sort of absolute vision, such as the Three Selfs and *kyosei*, which have viability lasting beyond the present age, that are required of the company." If Mitarai can harness his vision in the hearts of the employees, it should then be quite possible to sustain the sense of a common destiny that is at the core of Canon's philosophy and operations.

CONSCIOUSNESS MANAGEMENT

What Takeshi Mitarai accomplished by dint of personal charisma, Fujio Mitarai is intent on accomplishing through a return to the original traditions of the company and re-establishing even more strongly its basic principles. To achieve this, consistent communication of these principles within the company is required and Mitarai is working to establish a certain consciousness in top and middle-level management.

Putting top-down first

Of this top-down approach, Mitarai says: "The tasks of top management are to use their wits, decide on objectives, select strategy, and then take the lead in producing results. Naturally you listen to the opinions of the workers at the implementation stage, compare them with your own, and make whatever adjustments are needed. But it must be the top that develops the form of the framework. I have no need for managers who sit and wait for their staff to say something. This top-down approach may well have come from the

U.S., and I think it's just fine. If you wait until something happens from below, everyone else is going to get ahead of you. If you are going to rely on the brains of subordinates, it is better to promote them. It is managers who should be conscious of making the whole as good as it can be."

When Mitarai uses the term "top-down", he is referring not only to the leadership from the president and heads of business units, but also to that provided by middle management to their staff. While it is the top that determines objectives and strategy in broad terms, how that strategy is actually developed and advanced is influenced in no small way by opinions acquired through a bottom-up process. It is the same approach that Mitarai employed when the company eliminated unprofitable lines of business, and when the cell system was adopted.

There is another concept that bears Mitarai's hallmark: the condemnation of the practice of dumping a problem or task on someone else. For example, Canon led the camera industry by producing the lightweight and highly successful AE-1 SLR camera. This success was attributable to the use of plastic components, and the company started to include mold production in its contracts with parts vendors. In general, Canon uses a total of about 10,000 molds and dies, and relies heavily on outside suppliers. As a result, since Canon has no know-how in the field of molds and dies, it is not in a position to effect improvements in the speed of development or in cost savings. There is a hollowing-out effect, as value added has been moved outside the company. This passing of work to an outside party is not true rationalization.

"This passing on of responsibilities to create a participant is going on everywhere," Mitarai notes, pointing to the outsourcing in production and the preparation of design drawings as examples.

The president takes a hand in inhouse communication

"All you need at the workplace is that which is functional," Mitarai believes, and his office at the company headquarters overlooking the Tamagawa River gives a stark illustration of this. The room, which he took over after the death of Hajime Mitarai, is sparsely decorated and has changed little since he moved in. The one major change that Mitarai brought is a conference table, which is used for his frequent meetings with executives and employees, during which he uses a whiteboard. If only one person is visiting, they talk face to face across his desk. When the occasion demands, he will sometimes use strong language, but even a dressing down is done with both persons seated. His day is planned according to a schedule that is timed to the minute.

A typical day starts with the morning meeting — a tradition of more than 50 years' standing, having been initiated by Takeshi Mitarai. It is held at the same time every morning, in a room next to Mitarai's office. In theory, it is attended by everyone of director status and above, 17 people in all — but allowing for executives assigned overseas, there are normally about 10 in attendance on any one day. The objective of the morning meeting is to have an unreserved exchange of

Fujio Mitarai and Canon Inc. directors gather for their regular morning meeting

opinions and information. There is no agenda; attendees bring up whatever they feel needs to be discussed.

More than anything else, Mitarai values the morning meeting for its freedom of expression. Here, with the key executives present, they make decisions on everything from problems related to day-to-day business, deal with crises, and issue instructions on the basis of those decisions. Since the founding of the company, it has been a tradition at Canon to not use an internal memorandum for reporting on each morning's decisions. This whole arrangement functions well and Mitarai insists that it makes for better efficiency when the executives are also charged with implementation. For Canon's style of speedy business, the morning meeting is vital.

At least once a month, he uses his lunch break to hold a meeting with heads of operations, including accounting and human resources, and the top persons at headquarters units. In a small conference room next to the president's office, they get together and have "speak your mind" sessions.

Some have commented that before Mitarai took over, Canon had a dozen major divisions that operated like personal fiefdoms, obsessed with building sales numbers at any cost. Mitarai acknowledges the truth of this criticism and has worked hard to effect a change in this atmosphere. From the start of his presidency, Mitarai has taken the lead in improving internal communications, personally addressing the monthly meetings of up to 700 general managers.

As a rule, Mitarai visits every factory and office at least once a year. During such visits, he reviews the company's performance during the year and presents an overview of the outlook and long-term plans. "At small offices, I meet everyone; at large offices, I meet everyone of assistant manager status or higher; and at very large offices or factories, I have about a thousand persons get together, all managers, department chiefs or higher," Mitarai says. "I speak for about two hours each time. This way I talk directly to about 7,000 employees every year. I wish that I could speak to every single employee, but unfortunately that can't be done."

A typical day for Mitarai

7:20 a.m.
 Arrive at office, review in-basket; telephone president of European
subsidiary

7:50 a.m.
 Morning meeting

8:30 a.m.
 Hear reports on business activities, approve accounts settlements

9:30 a.m.
 Telephone calls to Operations heads

10:30 a.m.
 Approval of accounts settlements for subsidiaries

11:00 a.m.
 Working lunch; business strategy committee meeting

1:00 p.m.
 Approve accounting report, business operations reports

3:30 p.m.
 Government-related meeting

6:30 p.m.
 Telephone report from president of Chinese subsidiary

7:00 p.m.
 Dinner with customer

10:30 p.m.
 Return home

His time in the United States gave Mitarai broad experience
of working with people from a variety of backgrounds. This
taught him that there is little to be gained from following the
motto "Silence is golden". What matters more is to match words
with action. He says that it is not acceptable to rely on intuition
any more than on telepathy. Rather, it is necessary to use language that is easily understood, and explain things repeatedly so

that everyone involved can contribute their best efforts toward accomplishing one and the same objective. While Mitarai prefers direct, face-to-face communication, he also uses information technology to supplement this. "Ordinary communication makes for speed in management. Speed in communication reduces the number of meetings you have to hold," he says.

Exploiting intellectual assets: A specialty of the house

At the end of September 2001, Canon held more than 50,000 patents, both in Japan and in other countries. These, together with utility designs and trademarks, are the company's intellectual assets. Making good use of these assets is a special characteristic of Canon. The first of these intellectual assets came in September 1934, soon after the seeds of the company were sown. Goro Yoshida, one of the founders of the company, had made a prototype of a 35mm camera and filed an application for a utility design.

At that time, Leica was the world leader in the optical equipment field and held many patents for cameras. Thus, from the outset, Canon was faced with the major challenge of how to develop its own product without infringing on Leica's patents. This scenario was replayed when the company started work on copiers, an area in which Xerox held the patents.

Canon received its first patent during wartime, for a utility camera. Then, in 1946, it began the practice of giving awards to employees whose work led to company patents. This, in turn, led to further reward schemes and to the formulation of a set of rules for matters relating to the handling of patents and trademarks. Behind these steps to create and protect intellectual property was an understanding that this would have a direct effect on future development and competitiveness.

In the summer of 1960, Giichi Marushima, who was instrumental in refining the company's patent strategy and who became a senior managing director, was summoned to the personnel department to be told that he was being transferred from the camera plant at the corporate head office in Shimomaruko, Tokyo, where he was a trainee, to the Patent

Section of the Technical Department. Two people had just left the Patent Section and they were looking for a rookie to help fill the gap.

The Patent Section had only come into being that April, in response to a warning by Hiroshi Suzukawa, then a director and in charge of technology for the company, to the effect that patents and designs would become increasingly important to the company. (Suzukawa, who would later become known as the father of technology at Canon, was a graduate of the elite Tokyo Imperial University and had worked in high-level naval design projects during the war.)

Marushima's job at the time involved only the routine work of conveying documents between the company's engineers and the offices of the patent attorney that Canon used, and making tracings of engineering drawings for patent applications. This gave him the freedom to spend some time in the Technology Department's new Product Research Section, where top-flight engineers from many parts of the company were being concentrated to work on making copiers successful commercial products.

At that time, the name "Xerox" was synonymous with plain-paper copying. Xerox had more than 600 patents on technology for copying machines and, because it stuck to the policy of not licensing it to other companies, no one was able to develop look-alike copiers. Canon, therefore, had to engineer its way around Xerox patents if it wanted to compete.

Marushima pored over every one of the Xerox patents and discovered a way to get around them. The key, he decided, was to make a system that did not form an electrostatic latent image only by means of an electrical charge and exposure to light. The solution lay in covering the photoreceptor, which is exposed to light, with an insulating layer. Repeated experiments eventually led to a method of copying that was different from existing methods. It was called the NP method.

The first patent application for this electrophotographic copying machine was filed in Japan in July 1965, and the first NP patent award followed in October 1967. Marushima was one of the three persons named in the basic patent. In April of the following year, Canon made public the principle of the NP system. In 1970, the company rolled out its (and Japan's) first plain-paper copier using the new technology, the NP-1100.

"Later on," former-president Yamaji recalls, "Canon switched to a Xerox-like system." In the interim, the NP series was a major profit center for the company. When Canon announced the completion of the copier in 1968, Xerox requested permission to inspect it, in accordance with the terms of a prior confidentiality agreement. As it transpired, Xerox had not, in fact, signed the agreement but Canon allowed the inspection anyway.

On the basis of the information obtained during the inspection, Xerox then modified its own patent application with the intention of thwarting Canon's application in Japan. Wherever Xerox filed, however, the application was rejected. Nevertheless, in Japan there was a sense of alarm. Xerox also tried applying pressure to Canon's lawyers overseas. After a degree of maneuvering — and sensing some danger from Canon now that it held a number of copier-related patents — Xerox inquired about the possibility of a cross-licensing agreement with Canon. The idea of using patents and cross-licensing as a business strategy was one by-product of the Xerox saga.

When Marushima joined the new Patent Section in 1960, it comprised four people. With the growing importance of the power of patents, the Patent Department was formed in 1972, with Marushima as its first general manager. In 1989, the scattered activities related to intellectual assets were collected in a section in the newly created Corporate Intellectual Property & Legal Headquarters. The group executive appointed to head this new Headquarters unit was Marushima. He was now the executive producer for the systematic creation and utilization of intellectual assets. Trademark registrations in and outside of Japan currently amount to 22,000. Utility designs, in and outside of Japan, number 5,500. Income created by these assets during the first half of Canon's 2001 fiscal year came to more than ¥150 billion. In a given year, the company files about 10,000 applications in Japan, and is awarded

3,000 to 4,000 patents. In recent years, in the United States the company has received nearly 2,000 patents per year. Since 1984, Canon has boasted about the same number of patent registrations in America as IBM.

Technology transforms corporate assets

The Corporate Intellectual Property & Legal Headquarters now

has more than 400 staff. It is rare for a Japanese company to have such a large unit devoted to this area. The current group executive is Nobuyoshi Tanaka, who has a background in semi-conductor devices, and was a joint recipient of the Thirty-Seventh Okochi Memorial Pro-duction Prize in 1991, together with Tadahiro Ohmi of Tohoku University and Hajime Mitarai, for their work on the development and commercial appli-cation of BASIS, or Base Storaged Image Sensor. A prestigious award, this is given by the Okochi Memorial Foundation, an organization that is dedicated to the promotion of scientific technology for the development of industrial production.

A member of Canon's intellectual property division consults a file in the company's IP reference room

The staff of the Corporate Intellectual Property & Legal Headquarters are dispatched throughout the company.

These men and women may be assigned to the creation of intellectual assets from the technology in any of the business divisions or research centers.

They work proactively to discover the seeds of possible future patents that the researchers and engineers themselves may not even be aware of. In the same way that Marushima became one of the inventors of the basic copier patent, Shigeru Ohno, general manager of Corporate Intellectual Property & Legal Headquarters, has his name as one of the patent holders for the Bubble Jet printer.

For technology to be transformed into patents, engineers have to understand the cutting-edge technology under development, and produce documentation. Working with the development staff, the people from Corporate Intellectual Property & Legal Headquarters put the technology in written form. Between them, they churn out some 10,000 patent applications a year; that is, about 30 a day.

When a product is to be developed in a certain group, the work is divided into five phases: namely, DA, when the development concept is defined; DB, the production of component prototypes, to ascertain the functionality of major parts or components; DC, building a functional model, checking unit compatibility, and checking overall functioning of the designed product; DD, fabricating samples; and DE, trial production, to determine the total functionality of the product. Volume production is begun only after the DE phase. To be able to advance to the next phase, the project has to pass through a series of checks, including one to ensure that there is no possibility of infringing another company's patents. If it is thought likely that continued work would lead to an infringement, the patent team has to decide what to do about this, and work with headquarters on possible cross-licensing approaches.

"It would require an enormous sum for licenses if Canon had no intellectual assets of its own," Tanaka says. "While the intellectual assets have intangible effects that defy accurate measurement, the benefits obtained from them are immeasurable." In addition to being useful in the development of new products, they are valuable as weapons for keeping one step ahead of the opposition. Not only do high-quality patents discourage other companies from entering a particular field, they also provide useful leverage in reducing payments made as part of cross-licensing deals.

Canon reported consolidated sales of copiers in the term ending December 2000 of ¥823 trillion. Assuming for the moment that Canon had had no intellectual assets with which to make those copiers, it would have had to pay upwards of 4% of sales for the requisite technology. For copiers, this would mean payments of roughly ¥3 trillion. Consolidated operating profit would take a hit to the tune of 13%.

"Since Canon has accumulated such a rich portfolio of patents, we can call for any company that wants to work with us to enter into a cross-licensing agreement. We've entered the digital age and the range over which Canon's technology can be embodied in new products is being rapidly extended. We fully expect that companies with which we have had no prior relationship will attempt an attack on our position, using patents as ammunition. At such a time, our patent portfolio will come in handy," says Tanaka. For Canon, intellectual assets are a safeguard against such threats.

Patent strategy: An expanding role

Despite all this, Canon had a bitter experience in this field during the 1990s. Honeywell brought suit against six Japanese companies for infringing its rights to automatic-focus technology for single-lens reflex cameras. According to reports, Minolta paid a minimum of US$127 million to settle. Although Canon has not announced a specific figure, it is thought that it paid Honeywell nearly ¥700 billion.

A subsequent study of Honeywell's patents by Canon found a number of other product areas that had the potential to cause problems in the future. This led the company to enter into an agreement with Honeywell for rights to use an automatic-focus device in cameras from 1992 until the patent expires. Because of a confidentiality clause, Canon has not revealed details of the agreement, but it is understood that it is not for auto-focus technology alone.

While Japanese companies in general make little of intellectual assets, Canon stands out in this regard. Having launched successful challenges to the dominance of Leica, in cameras, and Xerox, in copiers — to the extent that Canon holds 8,000 patents related to digital cameras and 12,000 patents related to Bubble Jet printers — Mitarai has great confidence in the company's digital-photo operations, which combine digital and inkjet technology.

Canon has recently entered into a new area for producing patents — the business-model patents which have become popular in the United States.

5

Going Global

ANNOUNCING AMBITIONS

On October 2, 2001, Canon took a bold step. It hosted a reception in Tokyo to reveal its plans for its digital-photo business, pledging to become number one in the field. On top of that, the company announced two new digital cameras and a lineup of new inkjet printers.

More than 200 journalists attended the press conference, at which Mitarai was flanked by Tsuneji Uchida, the executive in charge of digital cameras; Teruomi Takahashi, the executive in charge of inkjet printers; and Haruo Murase, the president of Canon Sales, the domestic sales subsidiary. Mitarai explained the strategic importance of this marriage of the digital camera and the inkjet printer. He then unveiled the compact PowerShot S40 and the PowerShot S30 — small, stylish, high-resolution, user-friendly digital cameras. Both the 4 megapixel S40 and the 3.2 megapixel S30 contained the high-precision CCD element.

The Digital Ixus compact digital camera, which had been rolled out in May 2000, had been a smashing success, establishing Canon's lead in this field. Marketed in the U.S. under the PowerShot brand, the Digital Ixus 200 and 300 models enjoyed strong success in the market in early 2001.

Domestic shipments of digital cameras were now greater than shipments of conventional cameras and Canon looked forward to growth of the market in overall terms.

The new S40 and S30 models were somewhat larger than the Ixus, and loaded with new features, such as Internet connectivity and options for the shutter sound.

The new inkjet printers — under the Pixus brand name in Japan — came in eight models and offered high resolution and higher printing speeds than earlier products. Ink was released through nozzles at 20-micrometer intervals, an innovation that drew on Canon's expertise in high-precision processing and its experience in making semiconductors. The new models represented a significant improvement in quality and color matching, such that printed colors matched those seen on both digital camera and computer monitors.

At first glance, the new products seemed to be little more than refinements of earlier models. Rival makers were also pressing ahead with high resolution, high functionality and high speed, and the changes that Canon had made were not such that they would establish solid superiority over rival products.

What Canon did do, though, was to introduce a new technology that allowed a digital camera to be connected directly to an inkjet printer. Mitarai made sure that he was there in person to bang the drum for this innovative development. The new "direct print" technology enabled a digital camera to be connected directly to the printer by means of a cable. This permitted consumers to print their photos easily at home, without having to use a computer. The new digital cameras also provided Internet connectivity, which made it possible for users to print the contents of websites as well.

Canon used the term "home photo lab" to promote the new products, as it was now possible to print photos at home. The market for film for conventional cameras was controlled by a very small number of film manufacturers. Now, however, to print photos at home, camera owners would need Canon products in the form of consumable supplies such as ink and paper. There was no other company, anywhere, in such a position. None of the rival makers of digital cameras were strong in printers, and makers of printers had no digital cameras to offer, enabling Mitarai to boast, "Because we had made an early start in developing the technology for both digital cameras and inkjet printers, the 20,000 patents we accumulated were four times the number of our competitors." Canon had tilled the soil a long time, and now rich harvests were promised.

Until recently, Canon was the only company that had the products to make "direct print" printing possible. However, a new industry standard, called PictBridge, was introduced early in 2003 and allows compatible products to realize direct printing, regardless of brand. This should promote total market expansion, as well as influence competitive strategies. Canon will move a step closer to realizing a dream if it can get others to use its standard. When Canon can sell ink, paper and even content as part of its digital-photo business, it means a new business model. This is an enormous opportunity for Canon. By 2005, on a parent basis, it expects to make this into a ¥500 billion business, a figure given by Mitarai at a recent press conference. The company is currently active in three broad categories: office equipment, including copiers; industrial equipment, such as semiconductor production equipment; and consumer devices, such as cameras. To achieve this goal will require that digital cameras and inkjet printers, two mainstays of the consumer business, continue to grow.

The rapid appreciation of the yen in 1986 led to a sharp drop in the company's profitability. When this was then compounded by the deflating of the bubble in the Japanese domestic economy, the period from the mid 1980s to the mid 1990s turned into something of a "lost decade" for Canon. At the launching of the new products, however, Mitarai could afford to say with some confidence, "We've finally completed preparations, and Canon is moving forward."

BECOMING TRULY INTERNATIONAL

Mitarai's eyes were on the next objective — making Canon into a truly global company. Phase II of the Excellent Global Corporation Plan was about to be enacted.

Four issues are addressed in Canon's management planning for achieving these goals. "First of all, we must be number one in the world in all businesses we are engaged in. Second, we must create powerful R&D, which will give birth to new businesses. Third, the company must be in a strong financial condition. Fourth, our employees are to have a corporate culture that enables them to give their best," says Mitarai. To be tops in each field of endeavor echoes Jack Welch's aspirations for General Electric; the mention of ideals and fighting spirit is a significant Canon addition.

For 2005, the entire Canon group (global, consolidated) target is for ¥3.8 trillion in sales, with pre-tax profits from sales of 10% or more, and leverage (debt to total assets) not to exceed 3%. Given that in 2000 Canon's consolidated sales were ¥2.78 trillion, pre-tax earnings to sales were little greater than 8% and leverage was 14%, the targets for 2005 are quite ambitious. In effect, Canon has to add ¥1 trillion to sales

Consolidated Base Targets of the New Plan		
	2005	**2000 RESULTS**
Sales	¥3.8 trillion	¥2.78 trillion
EBT/Sales	10% or greater	8%
Shareholder's equity	60% or greater	48%
Leverage (debt dependency)	3% or less	14%
U.S. & Europe holding-company sales	¥1 trillion or more at each	US: ¥934 billion Europe: ¥768 billion
Sales ratio of domestic production companies excluding Canon parent company	50% or more	20%

over this five-year period. Given Japan's prolonged economic weakness, and the changed world outlook following the emergence of international terrorism, this will be no easy task.

Nevertheless, Mitarai is bursting with confidence, a confidence born of having implemented the first long-term plan for the company and having helped Canon recover from its "lost decade". "I have constantly insisted on consolidated management in order to implant the concept of total optimization, on using cash-flow management in order to make the company financially solid, and on thorough rationalization from development to production to distribution," says Mitarai.

Trilateral controls

If the sales target is to be achieved by 2005, it will be essential to start new lines of business and expand existing ones. The fundamental mechanism underlying the company's efforts in this regard is what it calls the "Three Regional Headquarters System," under which there are three key Canon companies — one in Japan, one in the U.S. and one in Europe. The European company, Canon Europe, is for the most part a marketing company, but it is to be made into a manufacturer that possesses R&D capability. Each of the three companies will have multiple responsibilities, according to Mitarai. Up to this point, Canon Japan has been the center for R&D and has created the seeds for new business. But now all three companies will vie for accomplishments within a framework of global management. If Phase II of the Excellent Global Corporation Plan is achieved as Mitarai expects it will be, Canon will be transformed into a truly global company with a solid foundation in three parts of the world.

The areas of development work will be adjusted to ensure that none of the three parts of the company is in direct competition with another. "The three are all to export, but to export products that differ, with each product representing the strengths of the originating region. Each company will be managed in such a way as to reduce foreign-exchange risk," says Mitarai. To facilitate a three-way adjustment process, Canon is considering the possibility of establishing a holding company that would be the global headquarters for the Canon group.

In moving towards establishing the Three Regional Headquarters System, in May 2001 Canon established a company in London to serve as the regional headquarters for the marketing subsidiaries in European countries. It started with about 150 development, managerial and other personnel, who were transferred from Japan or European subsidiaries. Plans were for it to be converted into a holding company, the timing coordinated with adoption of the euro in 2002. This company would take over Canon's interests in the 128 affiliated companies in Europe.

In the U.S., Canon U.S.A. is to be converted into a holding company and to acquire Canon's holdings in 34 U.S. affiliates. The number of affiliates dedicated to software development, now two, would be increased, and development of hardware would be added to activities in the U.S.

With the shift to holding companies in Europe and the United States, Canon plans a structural reform of the marketing activities in the countries under their respective jurisdictions.

The Three Headquarters System is also expected to bring about improvement in Canon's financial position. "Up to now," Mitarai says, "we could have an inefficient arrangement whereby one company with a surplus of capital puts it into a deposit-taking bank at low interest, while another company in the group is borrowing from a bank and paying high interest." The three headquarters will raise funds with greater efficiency, through closer liaison with each other and close monitoring of local conditions. By lending and borrowing among group companies, Canon will be able to reduce its dependency on banks. By these methods it will be better able to achieve the goal of reducing leverage to no more than 3%.

Accompanying implementation of the trilateral scheme is deployment of ¥1 trillion for long-term investment. The money is to be used largely by the Canon group companies for investment in R&D and acquisitions as means of acquiring technology. Even if the new American and European companies are equipped with a product or business development function, it is not to be expected that they will be able to yield meaningful results quickly. By using some ¥200 billion for M&A, mostly in the U.S., Canon plans to buy time for itself. As of the end of fiscal year 2002, Canon had a war chest of ¥520 billion of cash on hand and sales of ¥3 trillion. The funds to enable expansion through acquisitions were ample enough.

Domestic production affiliates also have a contribution to make in promoting Canon's diversification. The group includes five strong production companies, including Canon Finetech. These companies are capable of undertaking business development on their own, and have been given a mandate to do so. It is envisaged, in fact, that sales generated from business other than that within the parent company will grow from the present average of 20%, to 50%.

BREAKING NEW GROUND

Mitarai has his own three-part classification of the world's leading companies. They are the pure-plays; the conglomerates; and the intermediates, for which there is not yet a neater name. The pure-plays have a single focus. Toyota, General Motors, Dupont, IBM — these are pure-plays. Conglomerates are companies made up of companies that have no relation to one another except through capital. Mitarai cites General Electric as an example. And Sony, with interests that extend to entertainment, insurance and banking, is another of Mitarai's conglomerates. In between these two groups are the intermediates, which have various businesses that are related to one another but whose overall management is in the form of that of a conglomerate. Take, for example, a corporate group that has been developed on the basis of strength in technology. In such a group, some companies may be publicly owned. But rather than there being a vertical hierarchy of parent and subordinate companies, they are more like siblings. Such a group would be an intermediate. Hitachi and Toshiba are close to this model.

Which development path, then, should Canon take? Mitarai wants to take the third, the intermediate way. In the past, Canon would have been classified as a pure-play. Beyond the problem of a built-in limitation to future growth if Canon adhered to this, the risk of having to compete on a global scale would be immense. "It would not be suitable, from the viewpoint of Canon's history and corporate culture, to follow the path to becoming a conglomerate," says Mitarai. Therefore, the company is headed, he says, towards becoming a company that is managed in conglomerate manner but has constituent companies that are linked primarily by technology. Or, put differently, a company that has a federal type of management by means of the Three Regional Headquarters System that operates on a global scale. This means Canon will acquire companies that are technologically related to the Canon group's current activities as part of the growth and expansion process.

Having judged that the corporate group form taken by Hitachi and Toshiba, two highly diversified makers of electric machinery, doesn't match these times, Canon is moving in the direction of a corporate group of specialized companies that are tied to each other by technology. In January 2001, Mitarai set up the Management Strategy Committee, which cut laterally across business division lines. It was a new version of the Management Reform Committee that he had set up in 1998. Issues representing Mitarai's intended reforms, or issues he wishes to pursue, are in the purview of projects originating in the Management Reform Committee. This is because Canon adopted a matrix form of organization.

The project teams are called specialized committees. While the work of these committees is never fully disclosed — as to do so would reveal in detail the future directions the company will pursue — there has been continuous work on "finance" and "group logistics systems" within the committees, and there are many committees dedicated to technological matters. There are also indications that the areas of digital photography, next-generation steppers, CMOS sensors and NADA are on the agenda. There is also a committee dedicated to the Three Regional Headquarters System, which is chaired by Mitarai himself. If Canon is to succeed in its aim to become a global company, much will depend upon the effectiveness of the matrix method.

ACHIEVING BRAND CONSISTENCY

The Corporate Brand Management Committee was established in April 2001 with the task of achieving and maintaining tight control of Canon's corporate brands. Headed by Nobuyoshi Tanaka, head of the Corporate Intellectual Property & Legal Headquarters, this committee is responsible for controlling the use of logos and the company's name. It also analyzes and evaluates the group's brand images.

This committee has representatives from the likes of Corporate Communications Center, General Affairs Headquarters, Design Center, Corporate Planning Development Headquarters, as well as two divisions from the domestic marketing arm, Canon Sales, Communications Headquarters and General Affairs. The Committee forms working groups on an ad hoc basis, enlisting additional representatives of appropriate divisions when needed.

Three months earlier, a Brand Communications Center had been established within the Corporate Communications Headquarters, the hub of existing public relations activities. But the activities of the new center were given a twist. "Whenever we have a message from Canon, whether through advertising, events, the Internet, or other means, we want to add a little something so as to augment the brand value," says Tetsuo Hirasawa, the center's senior general manager. "You can see it from the history of Canon. Development of the company is also development of the brand." Hirasawa is hardly surprised by the recent boom in brand management in Japan because, from its inception, Canon has been oriented to building its brand name.

For 51 years, until 1988, the hawk was the symbol used to represent Canon.

It was only when the company began to make significant exports to the United States that Canon became hypersensitive to its brand. When Takeshi Mitarai negotiated a sales contract with the Bell and Howell company in 1950, his counterpart told him: "If this camera had not been made in 'Occupied Japan', but was a Bell and Howell product, it would sell like hotcakes." Japanese products then had the reputation of being cheap in both price and quality, so the outlook for selling a quality camera from Japan was dim. However, to Mitarai, selling the product under any other name would have been a sell-out, not a sales contract. The negotiations were halted. An opportunity was rejected in order to protect the brand.

Canon's plans to sell its cameras on the other side of the Pacific ran aground and, in 1966, at about the time Fujio Mitarai arrived in America, the brand names Yashica and Nikon were firmly entrenched. Starting in 1962 the company sold its cameras under the Canon brand through Bell and Howell, but had made scant progress in closing the gap that separated Canon from the other two camera-makers. Then, as Mitarai was heading home by taxi late one night, he saw the Yashica sign on the company's building on Queens Boulevard in New York City. He felt depressed, as Canon's failure to make any significant inroads into the American market was a cause of some concern and considerable bafflement given its status as one of Japan's major camera-makers.

In fact, it was not until the middle of the 1970s, after the sales agreement with Bell and Howell had ended and Canon began selling its own products, that the Canon brand became widely known in America. Significantly, in 1976 Canon released the first camera in the world to incorporate a microprocessor, the AE-1 — the first fully automatic SLR camera. This was a hit all over the world. At that time, Hirasawa was working for Mitarai in America. His job was to handle publicity and it was he who arranged for the first national-network TV commercial for the camera, which did much to make the brand known. "It was the success of the AE-1 that established the Canon name in the camera world," says Hirasawa.

The AE-1, launched in 1976, featured a built-in microcomputer

The basic pattern for developing the Canon brand was established when the company entered the copier business. In this case, the product was based on the company's own technology and use of the Canon brand benefited from the company's success in the camera business. In turn, the subsequent success of Canon's copiers served to reinforce the brand image with respect to cameras. This pattern was repeated when the company went into printers and, in time, the Canon corporate brand came to be associated with a variety of products and services in the optical and precision-engineering fields.

Needless to say, Mitarai has very strong views on the importance of the Canon brand, and has expressed these very forcefully on a number of occasions. In a presentation to the Nikkei Global Management Forum in October 2001, for example, he referred to the Canon brand as the jewel in the crown of trust that the company has accumulated over the six decades since it was founded.

In August 2001, *Business Week* magazine carried a special feature on the best global companies, in which the cash values of corporate brands were calculated and reported for the top hundred companies. There, in 41st place, was Canon, with a brand valued at US$6.6 billion. Basking in first place was Coca-Cola, boasting a brand valued at US$68.9 billion. Also ahead of Canon were a number of Japanese companies, notably Toyota, Sony, Honda and Nintendo. Nevertheless, Canon was still ahead of other well-known giants, including Pepsi Cola, Xerox, Gucci, Chanel, Boeing and Mobil.

In October of the same year, Kunio Ito, a professor at the Graduate School of Commerce, Hitotsubashi University, announced the results of work he had undertaken in conjunction with the Nihon Keizai newspaper group to develop a model by which to evaluate corporate brands. His Corporate Valuator employed independent variables such as evaluations of the influence of the corporate brand on customers, on employees, and on shareholders, and the discounted cash-flow method was used to measure the present value of brands from the cash flow that the brands would generate. When the various evaluations had been made, NTT Docomo came out on top, with ¥5.7 trillion. Canon's score of ¥1.1 trillion was good enough to earn it 10th place.

Taking Canon's share price at ¥4,000, the company's market capitalization is about ¥3.5 trillion. If the brand value as estimated by *Business Week* is converted at ¥120 per dollar, it would correspond to one-fourth of the market cap amount. In the other model, one-third is brand value. Though the methodology and definitions of the two approaches differ considerably, it is readily apparent that both point to the fact that Canon's brand value is high.

Brand management gets tougher

If Canon was performing so well, why had it chosen a few months earlier to set up a new organization to fortify its brand power?

One reason, of course, is to support Phase II of Mitarai's three-headquarters plans (Japan–U.S.–Europe). Mitarai's take on this is that the company is moving inexorably in a direction in which each of the three regions, on the basis of their identifying features, is to undertake business operations that exploit the technology most representative of each area, acting not at the direction of a head office, but by using their own capital and human resources for research and development, and for production of goods. Without a unifying corporate brand, there would be a danger that the three regions might diverge.

"With innovation and *kyosei* providing a foundation, the development of the Three Regional Headquarters System creates mutual respect for the individuality of each region," says Mitarai.

If there is success in technological development in accordance with Phase II of the Excellent Global Corporation Plan, the process of diversification will become stronger than otherwise.

Canon Trading, a sales subsidiary of Canon Sales, has undertaken the wholesale purchase of golf clubs for resale. In the past, these clubs bore the Canon brand and the Canon logo appeared on advertising flyers for the clubs. But the parent company objected. "It was because it was undesirable that the logo be used for a product that had no direct relation to the company's technology and principal business operations," Hirasawa says. Canon Trading is a directly owned subsidiary. But it was not Canon that made the golf clubs, nor was Canon technology used to design or produce them. The way the logo was used presented the danger that the product would be improperly perceived. Finally, as decided by Canon Sales, the handling of the product was changed.

While "Canon" represents the company's corporate brand, the company also has various product brands, such as "EOS" for SLR cameras. The authority to make the final decision on product names rests with the appropriate division at the Canon head office. Recently, however, marketing departments have had an increasing influence on product nomenclature. In November 2001, for example, following strong inhouse lobbying by Canon Sales, the inkjet printer previously known in Japan as Wonder BJ was renamed Pixus. The thinking behind this change was that Canon had slipped a little behind its nearest competitor and a change of name to accompany the updating of the product line was needed. (Product names comprising "BJ" followed by a number were retained for overseas markets.)

"Procter & Gamble and other international makers of consumer goods work with a multiple number of well-known brands as part of their diversified business operations; the value of corporate brands is high. Whether it is Canon for cameras or Canon for copiers, we have to tie the corporate brand to the product. It is going to be important from now on not to merely attach a message to a product, but for the corporate image to be formed by the totality of corporate behavior, including the company's management and corporate culture. Brand management is part of corporate management," says Mitarai.

A HISTORY OF INTERNATIONALIZATION

Canon achieved its growth, initially, through exports. In that sense, Canon has been an international company from an early date. Moreover, Phase II of the Excellent Global Corporation Plan is an extrapolation of this. In this light, it would be worthwhile to take a look at the history of Canon's international activities.

Representing Japan, the exporter nation

No fewer than five Japanese camera-makers exhibited at the international trade show in Chicago in 1950. Takeshi Mitarai was there as a representative of the camera industry. On arriving in Chicago, he was greeted by the news that Bell and Howell, the Chicago-based maker of movie cameras, was to have a new president, Charles Percy (who would later become a Republican senator and head of the Senate Foreign Relations Committee). Mitarai decided to meet with Percy.

Their first meeting took place at the office of Chicago's Chamber of Commerce. Mitarai showed Percy a Canon II B camera he had brought. "Tell me, without reservation, if this camera would be popular if sold in America. Don't hold back on the criticism," Mitarai said. Percy wouldn't give an immediate answer: "This looks like quite a camera, but I can't give you an answer right away. Give me a month." Mitarai handed over the camera and spent the month traveling around the United States to inspect modern factories, production equipment and machine-tool manufacturers, worrying about the expenses of hotels, meals and travel all the while.

The month passed, and Mitarai went back to Chicago for another meeting with Percy. Before Mitarai could say a thing, Percy told him, "My engineers say this camera is a couple of levels above a Leica." This was good enough to bring to an end any thoughts Mitarai might have been entertaining about allowing Canon cameras to be sold under the Bell and Howell name.

This meeting was to have a big influence on Canon's business strategy. Mitarai was concerned, as other Japanese were at the time, about changing the perception of "Made in Japan," from a label symbolizing products that were shoddy and cheap, to one that represented quality and value. After Mitarai returned from the United States, Canon got to work at getting into exports in a major way. Mitarai set about building a factory furnished with modern equipment in order to produce high-quality cameras. After looking at several possible sites, he chose a plant that had been operated by the Fuji Aeronautical Instrument company at Shimomaruko 3-1-2, in Tokyo's Ota Ward. (This is the location of the head office today.) The plant cost ¥90 million and a further ¥50 million was invested in modifying the building to ensure that the factory met the highest standards available at that time.

All the same, the company was chronically short of capital. On top of that, it had no channel for exporting its products. Then, out of the blue, came an approach from Jardine Matheson, the Hong Kong-based British trading company, which was interested in exporting Japanese cameras. It was said that Jardines' preferred source of supply was Nikon, but the trading company contacted Canon as well.

Canon's negotiation position called for a loan of US$300,000 as a condition for the provision of sales rights. Production output at the time was of the order of 1,000 cameras a month, and the contract provided that for five years, at least 70% of production would be sold to Jardines. But just before the signing of the contract, Mitarai made a bold, surprise move. To the manager of Jardines' Tokyo office Mitarai said, "We want to borrow US$500,000," a sum considerably higher than the one negotiated. "We will repay it without fail. Look me in the eye," he said. Fifteen seconds of absolute silence followed. Jardines' manager replied, "Okay." In that instant, Canon obtained the funds needed to develop an over-seas sales network. It was November 1951, and in the same month, the factory at Shimomaruko was completed.

Around this time, Canon also launched a technological and product attack. As a successor to the Canon II B, the company announced the world's first 35mm focal-plane-shutter cam-era, which had a contact for synchronization with a strobo-scope. In time, this camera — the IV SB — became recognized as a landmark in the history of Japanese cameras. Then, in December 1952, Canon brought out a 50mm F1.8 lens, which was superior to comparable German lenses, and priced it at ¥74,000. At this time Japan was busy producing goods for pro-curement by the U.S. in connection with the Korean War. Canon output rose to 2,000 cameras a month.

Advancing in overseas markets

In 1954, Canon completed repayment of the Jardines loan, well inside the five-year repayment period agreed. Then, shortly after the exclusive overseas sales rights agreement expired in June 1955, Canon opened an office in New York. At 550 Fifth Avenue, Tomomasa Matsui and five employees started work at breaking into the American market. With the encouragement of the Japanese government, which saw cam-eras as a means for earning hard currency, the industry had opened the Japan Camera Center in New York City. Despite this, however, Canon's camera sales did not grow. In 1958, as losses mounted, Canon ceased its marketing operations there, arranging for another company to handle sales on its behalf.

The turning point in Canon's fortunes overseas came in 1960, when Bell and Howell came back into the picture. The Chicago company approached Canon to ask if it could once again sell Canon's cameras. In 1961, Percy went to Japan and

In 1955 Canon opened its first U.S. office in New York

a sales contract was signed. American sales through Bell and Howell began in 1962.

When Takeshi Mitarai visited the United States for the first time in 1950, Canon's consolidated sales were ¥378 million. Camera sales accounted for 89% of that, at ¥337 million. The value of exports at this time was 77% of sales, or ¥289 million. From that time on, however, domestic demand in Japan zoomed, causing the share of exports sales to decline. The lowest point ever reached for the camera export ratio was in 1964, the year of the Tokyo Olympics. Domestic and export sales combined came to ¥15.8 billion, an increase of 42 times in 14 years. Of this sum, exports accounted for 3.9 billion, or 25%.

The New York branch was closed in 1965 and replaced by a new company, Canon U.S.A., the following year. Canon, trailing Nikon and Yashica, was shifting into a higher gear. As we saw earlier, Fujio Mitarai was among the vanguard sent out to man the new post. Despite the trials and tribulations he experienced, exports began to recover rapidly and, in 1967, reached the 50% mark. Part of the reason for this was the weak domestic demand that came with the recession that hit Japan after the 1964 Olympics.

Takeshi Mitarai, in his New Year's address to employees in 1967, gave them the slogan, "Cameras in the right hand, business machines in the left", and at the same time announced a target export ratio of 60%. His intent was to use the foundation that had been 10 years in the making to significantly increase export sales, especially to the U.S. and Europe. Business machines too made their contribution, and Canon's export ratio steadily rose. From 1976 onwards it was at the 60% level, and from 1979, the 70% level.

Expanding overseas production

If the first phase of Canon's internationalization is attributed to the expansion of exports under Takeshi Mitarai, the second phase began with the introduction of production overseas, under Ryuzaburo Kaku, the company's third president.

The second year of Kaku's presidency, 1979, corresponded with the fourth year for the Premier Company Plan. Overseas sales on a consolidated basis passed the ¥1.3 trillion mark. But the rise in exports from Japan during this time had been so strong as to create trade friction between Japan and its trading partners. Criticism of the Japanese seemed to escalate, from a focus on textiles in the 1960s, to steel and TVs in the 1970s. When the Premier Company Plan was first conceived, Kaku felt that economic friction overseas would become a deterrent to corporate growth. Basic to the plan was an organization based on business activity divisions, but a second key part of the plan was internationalization.

Kaku's strategy was to make investment a high priority in countries where a problem was likely to occur. On this basis, he decided to invest in France and, in August 1983, Canon France Bureautech (today, Canon Bretagne) was established, with capital of 40 million francs. In 1985 Canon went to the U.S., and Canon Virginia was established for the development and production of office-automation equipment in the United States.

In Asia, Canon already had a presence in Taiwan, where it had established in 1970 the company's first overseas venture. In 1984 Canon entered into a technical tie-up with the government of mainland China. This tie-up led to the production of copying machines in the Chinese cities of Zhuhai and Tianjin. In 1985 Canon started a joint venture in Korea with the Lotte group, called Lotte Canon. Three years later, in 1988, the establishment of Canon Opto (Malaysia) marked the company's advance into Southeast Asia. In 1989 Canon Dalian Business Machines was established as another undertaking in China.

In September 1985, representatives of the world's leading economies met at the Plaza Hotel in New York, and signed what is known as the Plaza Accord. They agreed to intervene in the foreign-exchange market in order to adjust currency exchange rates, and bring down the value of the dollar. As a consequence of the meeting, the yen began to climb, causing a recession in Japan. Although in the process of expanding overseas production, Canon was still reliant on exports, and the yen's rise dealt a body blow to earnings — as it did for many major Japanese companies. Recurring profit in 1986 declined for the year by 69%, a full ¥13 billion. This even included collecting dividends from overseas subsidiaries as a means of propping up parent-base earnings.

In April 1986, Kaku revealed a strategy for dealing with the challenge of the stronger yen. The company would raise prices in dollar regions, expand sales volumes, and relentlessly cut costs, he said, as well as increase imports of parts from Taiwan and other Asian countries.

In 1986 Canon contracted for a transfer of its entire production of handheld calculators to Kinpo Electronics, in Taipei. Canon would continue to control design, technical supervision and quality inspections, and all products would be sold under the Canon brand, but every single calculator would be made in Taiwan. Parts and labor were less expensive in Taiwan than in Japan and, equally important, the New Taiwan dollar was linked to the American dollar. Thus, in net terms, production costs were reduced by about 30%.

Part of the rationale for this was to do something about aggressive price slashing by Casio. But when the company elected to transfer production in its entirety to an offshore factory, rather than dealing with the challenge by piecemeal efforts such as cutting the cost of a part here and a part there, it created a sensation in Japanese industry.

Domestic prices had already been reduced in October 1985, right after the yen began to appreciate. To cover this, Canon increased export prices on its cameras, copiers and facsimile machines by between 5% and 10%. This was not enough, however, because it proved difficult to carry the increases over to sales prices in the United States. Fujio Mitarai, who was president of Canon U.S.A. at the time, recalls, "It was painful, as the strong yen raised the import price but the ceiling for market prices couldn't be raised any higher."

When the yen–dollar exchange rate reached 150 in 1987, the company embarked on a campaign it called "Challenge 150", which was intended to make Canon capable of competing at that exchange rate. Executives and managers took pay cuts, vendors were requested to lower their prices, and production at factories in Germany, France, the United States, Italy and elsewhere was increased.

But the yen strengthened even more in the 1990s, and seemed to become entrenched at the 100 level. Hajime Mitarai, then president of the company, issued instructions to all members of the Canon group, to implement the "211 Vision", a reference to the desired ratio of destinations for shipments from domestic factories: for every two products to be shipped to domestic resellers, one would be sent to Europe and one would be sent to the United States. As of December 1992, the export ratio, which had been 80%, was reduced to 50%, and the overseas production ratio was increased from 25% to 50%.

The expansion of domestic sales as a means of lowering the export ratio was made a business objective. Canon's annual sales were around ¥1 trillion. To reduce exports from 80% to 50% while maintaining the same level of sales would require an increase of some ¥300 billion in domestic sales. As a further cost-cutting exercise, and to improve communications with development managers, in August 1993, the executives moved from their offices in Shinjuku, located in downtown Tokyo, to the Shimomaruko building, in a more rural area of the capital.

Kaku, Yamaji and Hajime Mitarai had each played their hands. Despite their prodigious efforts, the strong yen resulted in stagnant earnings for Canon for a period of some 10 years starting in 1985. This was to weaken the company financially.

The continuing challenge of foreign exchange

Canon's consolidated sales in 2000 were ¥2.8 trillion. Of that sum, overseas sales were ¥2 trillion, or 71% of total sales. The Americas, with the United States accounting for the majority share, provided ¥934 billion, and European sales were ¥768 billion. A change of one yen either way in the yen–dollar exchange rate would have produced a change in annual sales of ¥11 billion, and of ¥4 billion in annual pre-tax earnings, all other conditions being unchanged. Similarly, a change of one euro would have altered the figures for sales by ¥7 billion and earnings by ¥4 billion. This is a tricky business and Canon's foreign-exchange challenge continues to this day.

Once a month, Canon's executives get together for a conference. At this meeting, Toshizo Tanaka, group executive for the Finance & Accounting Headquarters, outlines his forecast for currencies in the coming three months and what hedging strategy to take.

As its basic method of hedging, the company uses only forward contracts and covers half of its requirements of dollars and euros for the coming three-month period. The other half is not hedged, except when necessary, at the spot rate (the spot rate is the latest rate). "If the entire amount is hedged, arbitrary judgments come in. So we opt for the midway point," says Tanaka.

At present, if there is a major difference between actual settlement rates and the forecast rate, shipment prices are adjusted; this is done at intervals of three months. A variation of just one yen from the forecast rate, of course, has great impact on the bottom line. For this reason, at the monthly meeting, Tanaka also explains how currencies have performed in the recent past, how they have varied from the forecast rates and the effect of the variation.

When Fujio Mitarai became president and CEO in 1995, he came to the job after Canon had experienced its "lost decade", which came about as a result of excesses in organizing the company into business divisions and problems with the currency exchange rates. He has made steady progress in tackling the first of these problems by taking the company out of unprofitable business lines and reforming production methods. But, as yet, there has been no breakthrough with regard to the second challenge.

The real protection against the vagaries of exchange-rate volatility, in Mitarai's view, is a managerial structure that has the strength to withstand change in the external environment. That performance has improved since 1995 in the face of the strong yen reflects the strong influence of Mitarai. In the process of the overall transformation of Canon required in today's global environment, Mitarai has overseen the expansion by American and European subsidiaries acting on their own, and the company has become better at managing foreign-exchange risk. If the three regional headquarters each become more adept at continuously improving cash flow in the local currencies, in real terms, profits will remain rock-solid, notwithstanding any exchange-rate-induced changes in the apparent profits.

6

The Meaning
of Canon's
Transformations

Canon's transformations really began in 1995 when Fujio Mitarai became president and CEO. Mitarai's first move on his return to Japan from the U.S. was towards implementing strategies to correct the excesses that had arisen as a result of organizing the company along business-division lines. He also sought to strengthen cash-flow management by improving the return on assets and, thus, to establish a strong profit orientation.

The adoption of a consolidated performance-based system changed the relationships business groups shared with the head office and group companies.

Dropping out of unprofitable business lines such as personal computers was a form of shock therapy that reinforced the message that the company was no longer prepared to pursue unprofitable business lines. This new emphasis on cash flow was further underlined by a move away from conveyor-belt-based mass-production methods to a cell-production system, which had the beneficial effects of helping to prevent excessive output and reducing inventory.

In extending the production methods across the company, Mitarai was forced to dismantle the barriers that had been an unexpected and unwanted by-product of the way that the company had been organized into various business divisions. Under his guidance, the work of the Management Reform Committee, and deliberate steps to embed more horizontal communication channels, acted as a counter to the well-established vertical divisions and made for a more cohesive whole. At the same time, the organization's R&D activities were also given a shake-up as Canon pursued its key-technology policy.

While overseeing these transformations, Mitarai has also made progress in modifying the corporate culture so that Canon's long-standing principle that all employees should feel that they share a common destiny could coexist comfortably with the company's meritocratic approach. In doing this, he has sought to reinforce the founding principles of the company as embodied in the Three Selfs concept, and reaffirm its commitment to lifelong employment.

In 2001 Canon entered the second phase of its transformation. The war chest of reserves that had accumulated as a result of Mitarai's reforms was tapped for aggressive entry into new business areas, and on an international scale.

Canon's transformation has consisted of a rejection of a part of its past, and a parallel, sustained movement forward on the basis of those aspects of the past it chose to retain. This can be summarized as follows:

Making things

Reform　Conveyor-belt assembly ⇒ cell production
Progress　Domestic production ⇒ cell production; process industry

R&D

Reform　Proprietary technology ⇒ proprietary development + alliances with others

Inability to cease R&D efforts leading nowhere ⇒ taking inventory of R&D

Misuse of liberties ⇒ organization, orderliness

Progress   Circulating technology ⇒ use of key technology; constructing tech platforms

Teamwork ⇒ KI activities

Corporate culture

Reform   Vagueness, mutual dependency ⇒ consolidated cash-flow management; profit-orientation

Passing duties on to others ⇒ assumption of responsibility

Progress   Affirmation of meritocracy, health-first, neo-paternalism

Affirmation of the Three Selfs concept

Maintenance of lifelong employment

THE MANAGERIAL OPERATING SYSTEM

What becomes clear from this list is that the Canon transformation is rooted in an overarching management philosophy and its practical applications. Mitarai has employed a traditional Japanese management paradigm — lifelong employment — as his managerial operating system, while going to overseas sources for its applications in the areas of cash-flow and supply-chain management.

What sustains the lifelong-employment arrangement is the awareness of sharing a destiny. This, married to meritocracy, creates an energy that flows upwards from below. Because a large number of employees have a common focus, the chances of them scoring with a hit product are much higher. And if they fall short of coming up with a smash success, they still may hit a single or a double.

A managerial operating system must be coherent if it is to make up a workable whole. It would be dangerous to patch together elements of the American venture-business system and Japan's penchant for favoring large companies. To take a gamble like an American-style start-up — namely take a make-or-break gamble on a technology or strategy — is not suitable for large companies like Canon, as it would place the jobs of a large number of employees at risk.

On the other hand, it would be equally dangerous for a company to espouse the creation of shareholder value if the management refused to take responsibility for poor performance or for any subsequent reorganization — including the unpleasant business of having to lay people off — that might result.

For a company that desires to apply the peculiarly Japanese principle of group dynamism, and to promote the notion of a shared destiny, it would be counterproductive to talk of cutting employees. But to advance towards a goal while championing lifelong employment makes for an easily understood and smooth-functioning system.

A Japanese style of operating that revolves around the principle of lifetime employment has its own share of problems. However, these problems are surmountable. As Mitarai puts it, such a system can function well if the seniority system — with its stultifying reliance on others to make decisions — is uprooted and replaced by meritocracy, and if there is a willingness to end unprofitable operations. Japanese group dynamics are part of the fabric of society. Unraveling Japanese-style operating systems could have wide social consequences. "What is the best method in today's Japan to increase turnover and improve management efficiency?" asks Mitarai.

In many respects, Mitarai's approach is very similar to that adopted by Nissan chief executive Carlos Ghosn: installing an internal check function through consolidated cash-flow management and eliminating whatever holds down return on capital. Ghosn, too, has closed unprofitable factories and joint ventures in order to raise capacity utilization and free up capital.

There are similarities too in the respective operating systems. Ghosn also attended the Nikkei Global Management Forum in October 2001, and spoke about leadership. "The fundamental challenge in the reform of Nissan," he told the audience, "was to transform the corporate culture." In order to provide incentive to change, Ghosn undertook a review of the seniority system and replaced it with a results-based system of promotions.

In placing merit at the base of corporate culture, Ghosn was acting in the same way as Mitarai. But there is one major difference between the two approaches. While Ghosn sees a reduction in the number of workers as a natural consequence of plant closures, this is not the Canon way. Ghosn's approach has been to provide opportunities for younger employees. In doing this, he had no intention of maintaining any notion of a shared destiny for all employees, whatever their age.

Japan has many companies that have built up a superior workforce, a powerful technological base, and a body of expertise on the production floor. In the early 1990s, companies in the United States and elsewhere professed an admiration for the Japanese style and were studying Japanese management methods. Now, however, Japan has lost its self-confidence. While the prolonged economic downturn doesn't warrant optimism, the pendulum has swung too far in the opposite direction. It would be preferable to stay objective. Indispensable for this would be to perform radical surgery on business processes to eliminate inefficiencies, such as by abandoning unprofitable business operations. It is necessary to greatly tighten control and introduce measures such as consolidated cash-flow management.

Both large and mid-sized Japanese companies are now busily installing the most up-to-date American application software, while maintaining their Japanese-style operating systems. Canon has proved that this combination can work.

CONSOLIDATED CASH-FLOW MANAGEMENT

It is consolidated cash-flow management that has enabled the twin strands of meritocracy and lifetime employment to spread within the corporate culture.

The essence of cash-flow management, namely giving emphasis to balancing cash outflows and inflows, intrinsically provides a measure of the effectiveness of investment, and tends to eliminate or reduce unproductive fixing of capital. Cash flow is not improved simply by ensuring the smooth functioning of the equipment, however; the product has to be sold. It is meaningless to the company as a whole if cost reductions are concentrated at the factory as a partial optimization. Cash-flow management is a system that seeks overall optimization.

The introduction of the cell-production system by Canon is a classic example of cash-flow management in action. When the conveyor-belt assembly system was used, a substantial period of time was needed to change from making one product to making another. This was because of the time needed to change all the equipment and tools on the line. Then, once production had begun, it was difficult to stop it. The changes all along the line cost so much that they eliminated the profit expected from the product, and there was always a danger that this could result in a net loss.

With the cell system, loss of production time and costs incurred whenever there is a changeover to a different product are kept to a minimum. To minimize the possibility of making too many products, it is necessary to link production to supply-chain management, and to adjust production volumes to react sensitively to changes in sales. The cell system is particularly good at this. As we saw, too, work space requirements are reduced, as is investment in tools and assembly equipment, while warehouse requirements are also lowered.

Mitarai understood that cash-flow management makes for lean management and went about introducing his reforms at a furious pace. The subsequent turnaround in the company's operations would not have happened had it clung to the profit-and-loss accounting methods.

The cash-flow management methods were also applied to the research labs, where it is much more difficult to assess how quickly this would result in income. Canon still doesn't have an answer to this question because, in some cases, it may take 30 years to obtain meaningful results, as was shown in the search for and application of artificial fluorite. If such seeds were to be discarded in the name of short-term efficiency, the ability to generate positive cash flow over the medium and long term would be lost. When, however, the research bears fruit, the company ensures that it gets maximum benefit by circulating the resultant technology throughout the organization.

Reducing financial monkey business

When times get tough for a company in Japan, one method that some resort to is the dubious technique of transferring problems to subsidiaries. Called *tobashi*, the method became widely known in the late 1990s, when major Japanese securities brokers were found to have covered client losses by transferring unprofitable trades in this way. *Tobashi* involves, for instance, the transfer of excess inventory to a subsidiary, thus reducing the cost of inventory in the accounts of the parent company, assuming the company doesn't produce fully consolidated accounts.

When the economy is good, the subsidiary will be able to sell the goods. When the economy is bad, however, the subsidiary may be unable to sell the inventory and is forced to record a loss.

This sort of pattern could be seen frequently among large and mid-sized companies when the recession became prolonged. When top decision-makers concentrate only on problems at the parent company, in the end the entire structure is likely to crumble.

Consolidated management, on the other hand, refers to a method of corporate management that embraces the entire group.

Canon's adoption in 1997 of consolidated accounting for business performance of its operations divisions served to embed consolidated management thinking at that level of the organization. Performance evaluation was expanded from the level of individual groups to encompass the entire corporate group, including sales subsidiaries. The top person in each group became responsible for checking on sales trends at both domestic and overseas subsidiaries. In the past there were instances when inventory was built up at subsidiaries at the end of the fiscal year as a means of ratcheting parent sales upward, but such clever tactics ceased to be attractive when consolidated accounting was used. It came to be that factories made decisions based on a balanced overall perspective, taking into account the increase in overseas production as well as sales trends. These arrangements were given even wider scope in 2000, when Canon began to calculate balance sheets and statements of cash flow for each Operations division.

Simultaneous with the start of consolidated reporting, Canon introduced a system of diversified evaluation of consolidated performance. Applicable to all Operations and to all group companies, it provided a scorecard that included, but went beyond, profitability and other financial metrics to cover technological strength, new product development capability, quality levels, manpower efficiency and other indicators. This enables discovery and analysis of existing conditions, and problems, at the Operations and group company levels.

A large number of Japanese companies have been accustomed, for years, to using as the primary performance indicator the profits taken from the profit-and-loss statement for the parent company. While a start has been made towards convergence in the direction of internationally accepted accounting standards and the use of consolidated cash flow, these have yet to become well established. Canon is a leader in this respect.

Environment-related measures

Canon also carries out its environment-related activities from the standpoint of consolidated cash-flow management. The concept of *kyosei* — living and working together for the common good — had been extended to include environmental considerations before Mitarai became chief executive, but he has succeeded in incorporating such ethical concerns into his overarching guideline for maximizing the productivity of resources. The adherence to economic reason now guides the company's approach to addressing environmental problems.

At the company's Ami Plant, located about 60 kilometers north of Tokyo, where copying machines are produced, the shift to cell production in 1998 resulted in both cost reductions and environmental benefits in the form of reduced use of air-conditioning equipment and, through that, a decline in the plant's electricity consumption. As of the end of 2000, the benefit was an estimated reduction of 8,000 tons in carbon dioxide emissions, which is up to 7% of greenhouse gases generated by Canon.

Canon's approach to environmental management seeks to minimize the impact on the environment while, at the same time, maintaining growth in its operations.

In January 2001, Canon established a Global Environment Promotion Committee to coordinate the Canon group's environment-related activities. Managing director Yusuke Emura serves as group executive in charge of the company's Global Environment Promotion Headquarters, which comes under the direct responsibility of the president. The six heads of Operations divisions sit on this committee, which seeks to ensure that environmental considerations are treated as part of business strategy from the conceptual stage. The committee provides basic orientation in environmental matters for the entire corporate group. It has within it two subcommittees; one that focuses on products and the environment, and the other on production and the environment. There is an environment committee in each Operations division, and it is charged with coming up with concrete environmental measures that match the strategies of the division.

Having the heads of each Operations division participate in the decision-making process from an early phase, and having each of the divisions separately responsible for environmental affairs, has resulted in earlier formulation of environmental plans, while also contributing to the objective of promoting competition between divisions. Since 2001, an environmental item has been included in the consolidated performance evaluation, and performance in environmental matters has been made a part of performance evaluation.

Several committees have also been established to deal with specific problems. These committees, for example, deal with issues related to the design and manufacture of products that are easy to recycle, and with matters relating to the handling of chemicals. They take the initiative in contacting the appropriate divisions to inform, to raise issues and to prompt action in their respective areas of responsibility. They also promote group-wide measures in their respective fields.

Making effective use of capital

The shareholder equity ratio at Canon at the end of the 2000 fiscal year was 46% and debt dependency was 14%. These represent large improvements; compare the figures to those for 1995, before the kickoff of the Excellent Global Corporation Plan. Then, the equity ratio was 35% and debt dependency was 34%. In Phase II of the plan, that is from 2001, the equity ratio is to be raised to 60% or higher, and debt dependency reduced to 3% or lower. The plan is a blueprint for what would be an astonishing improvement of financial conditions. The surplus profit per share in 2000 was ¥974. This was more than eight years' worth of the earnings per share (diluted) for 1996–2000, or ¥119. As one result of the amazing increase in profits after 1995, the ratio of profits to shareholders' equity was lifted from 5%, the average for 1991–95, to 10%, for 1996–2000.

Overseas sales for Canon are more than 70% of consolidated sales. By extension, we can say that more than 70% of the company's earnings is vulnerable to changes in the value of the yen. About a third of consolidated sales are in the United States and if the yen-dollar rate moves by one yen it makes a huge difference. The same for Europe, which accounts for just under a third of consolidated sales. The most rational means for providing the company with the ability to accommodate this kind of currency exchange risk is to use profits to build up reserves and reduce leverage. This makes for a company that the owners can consider to be safe.

And yet the stockholders will find such an effort to build equity less attractive. This is because of the desirability of recycling a part of profits to the owners. The annual dividend in 2000 was ¥21 a share, an increase of ¥4 over the dividend paid in 1999. The payout ratio nevertheless was only 13%. The payout ratio averaged 29.7% during 1991–1995, but in 1996–2000 it declined to 15%. Judging from the payout ratio, the owners are not getting as large a share of profits as they might expect.

Mobilizing surpluses to build equity is the same thing as to reduce dependence on external finance. As far as stockholders are concerned, however, it would be perfectly acceptable to use external finance if the return exceeded the cost of that capital, thereby increasing the value of the company and, indirectly, the market capitalization, all this leading to an increase in dividends paid.

One measure of the value of a company is its notional takeover price: the sum of market capitalization and interest-bearing liabilities, from which liquid assets are deducted. The price of Canon, in 1991, was ¥1.2 trillion; in 1999 it had risen to ¥3.5 trillion. The notional price, however, declined by 4% in the following year, to ¥3.4 trillion in 2000.

BOTTOM-UP AND TOP-DOWN

The driving force in Japanese management has been the power derived from adopting a bottom-up approach that starts from the production floor. Japan has been viewed as deriving strength from its focus on the group, and from the ancient idea of group harmony, known as *wa*. During the 1980s, efforts were made in the United States to study the secret of Japan's strength, and some companies adopted Japanese management methods. The Six Sigma philosophy that General Electric is now deploying was developed as an imitation of

Total Quality Control, which is a Japanese contribution to quality control.

In Japanese management systems, it is production workers who take on the key roles in corporate reform. Employees are empathetic to reforms that originate and move from the bottom upward. Such production-level changes and improvements are an important part of the transformation at Canon. Without them, the story of Canon's transformation would be short indeed.

There is a limit, however, to the power derived from such bottom-up contributions. During the economic downturn that dominated the 1990s, many Japanese companies attempted to harness the power of bottom-up change. Hardly any of these efforts produced major results. What frequently happens is that reforms initiated at the production level bring only limited improvements. In comparison, U.S. companies engage in more radical reform, such as selling off entire divisions and laying off large numbers of workers at a time.

Within the organizational framework of Canon's business divisions, the power of bottom-up change was assigned high importance up to the middle of the 1990s. At the production level, each unit worked at developing its own new products and, if one of them was successful, the company made money. Canon was an innovative company but was also a classic example of one managed along traditional Japanese lines. It scored with some really big hits in the copier and printer fields, and because it developed new markets with these products, performance steadily improved without it being felt that there was any need to achieve overall optimization. This pattern disintegrated during the first half of the 1990s, however. Even if the company had a hit product, it brought little improvement to the bottom line.

It was at this point that Mitarai arrived on the scene. Where bottom-up had been the favored mode, he brought in a strong top-down approach. He put a stop to the piecemeal reform. He provided a unified direction for all employees. At the same time, he cleared the air within the company so that information could flow freely, maintaining the spirit of a common destiny sustained by the practice of lifetime employment.

Many people have participated in Canon's revitalization under Mitarai, and there are many stories to be told. But the most important factor in all of this has been Mitarai's deep involvement in every aspect of the transformation. It is because of this involvement at the top that the force for reform has penetrated the entire organization.

Reforms in the production and development areas began to make progress when the drive for overall optimization was announced. Activity in the operating divisions too was changed by the drive for overall optimization. The transformation, without doubt, was a revolutionary advance for Canon. But, at the time of writing, the transformation is but half complete. A more correct observation might be that the transformation has reached the threshold of becoming permanent. Midway, bottom-up change and top-down change meet and coalesce, and the resistance and friction generate the primary energy that drives the development of the company.

There is no "absolutely new model" for the mode of controlling a company. The environment in which the company finds itself, the abilities of the company itself, health conditions, relations to rivals and more are in constant flux.

In the future, Canon may come to show different management styles at the three regional headquarters companies. What is important is that momentum not be lost, and that overall controls are maintained, and that there is the capability to react swiftly to unexpected change.

FUTURE CHALLENGES

How much can Japan compete, sandwiched between China and the United States? We must also consider whether Canon's transformation will succeed or will fail in this respect.

There are varieties of capitalism. National and regional characteristics of capitalism have evolved, and American,

Japanese, North European, German, French and other styles can be discerned. Most recently there has been the emergence of the Chinese style of capitalism. Even while China continues to keep its socialist framework, it has begun to develop its own brand of capitalism. Japan is now being buffeted from both sides, by American capitalism and Chinese capitalism.

There are two characteristics of American-style capitalism to be noted here: management systems dedicated to creating shareholder value, wherein the shareholders are accorded the highest priority, and the venture capital system that created start-up companies, such as those in Silicon Valley. A typical example of the first would be Jack Welch's approach at General Electric, namely the disposing of many unprofitable divisions within GE. In the latter, innovation thought to be the key to fabulous income is linked to stock investment and increased America's competitiveness in the technology area. Both systems presuppose a high mobility of labor. They are parts of a society where wholesale firings, or layoffs, and continual changes of occupation are taken for granted.

America derives strength from the support for technology given through a linkage of academia, industry and government. The huge mirror telescope in Hawaii, the Subaru, is often mentioned by Mitarai in this context. Canon supplied some of the lens elements, and most of the entire telescope has been made by Japanese companies. The main lens element, however, is from Corning, and Corning has accumulated a good deal of its basic technology through academia-industry-government cooperation for the space shuttle. American patents dominate such areas as information technology and biotechnology.

Many American companies are oriented to the domestic market and domestic demand, because the scale of the domestic economy is so great. From 1985, however, the number of companies shifting to a global orientation increased. This globalization of American companies necessarily led to proselytizing on behalf of American capitalism. As far as American companies are concerned, the spread of American styles overseas makes it that much easier to do business, and the existence of different styles, such as that of Japan, are best eliminated. Now Japanese companies are being obliged to rethink the management methods they have used to date.

On the other side, China is battling Japan's manufacturing industry, using as its chief weapon low production costs made possible by low labor costs. China has learned of quality control from Japan and others, and has improved product quality at a remarkable pace. Previously, it had been thought that high value-added products would continue to be made in Japan, but now the number of quality products being made in China is on the increase. The impact of this buildup of productive capacity is being felt by Japanese manufacturing, and by the electrical machinery industry in particular.

Will Japanese companies perish under the pressure from Chinese and American styles of capitalism? Mitarai is forthright on this subject. "We must study what kind of work will survive in this country. We must maintain the R&D that is the driving force of what will enable Canon to survive, and by means of research and development we must create new businesses that have higher value-added content," he says. The transformation of Canon thus far has equipped it to aim at that target.

Business is to be expanded in Japan, in America and in Europe across the board. Canon in America and in Europe will not be dependent on the company in Japan; each is to undertake business independently. The outlook for Canon, caught between the capitalist styles of China and the U.S., is uncertain. What will be needed is the control to accomplish overall optimization for the three regional centers. Will Mitarai's style of combining a Japanese spirit and Western knowledge be accepted in the world and will Canon become a truly global company? The transformation of Canon is still in progress, but it has the potential to offer the world a new global management model.

7

An Interview with the President

LOOKING AHEAD

In October 2003, the respected Japanese business newspaper *Nikkei Industrial News* asked the presidents of 137 major Japanese companies to select the best among their ranks. In a front-page article on October 30, the newspaper revealed the results of its poll: Canon's president and chief executive Fujio Mitarai topped the list, well ahead of better-known leaders such as Nissan Motor's president Carlos Ghosn, who was second, or Toyota Motor's president Fujio Cho in third place. With typical humility, Mitarai said the selection was a great honor and refused to take personal credit for the recognition, saying it belonged to everyone at Canon.

Mitarai takes such accolades in his stride. As far as he's concerned, as long as personal tributes contribute to Canon's bottom line, he's all for them.

On November 4 2003, Mitarai took part in an hour-long interview at Canon headquarters for the purposes of this book. Mitarai looks much younger than his 68 years, with a round face that is almost completely unlined and only streaks of gray in his hair. While speaking, he is calm but sometimes gestures to make points.

CANON'S MANAGEMENT STYLE

Q: *Canon is a global corporation with operations in Japan, the U.S. and Europe. How would you describe your style of management?*

A: One phenomenon in Japanese industrial circles that annoys me is rendering in English words for management methods that have long been practiced in Japan and speaking of them as if they were new. Corporate governance is one example. Corporate governance has been practiced in Japan for a long time.

Today Japanese companies described as practicing U.S.-style management claim to have instituted a system of oversight through the introduction of independent directors. But in reality they have used a U.S.-style Japanese management model. It is not a U.S. model, because if it were truly U.S.-style management, and the board comprised, say, 10 members, at most three would be from the company — the CEO, COO and CFO. Even two, the CEO and COO, would be sufficient. So two or three would be from the company and the bulk — seven or eight — from elsewhere. That is the U.S. style.

But in Japan, U.S.-style management means equal numbers of directors from the company and from the outside. Even Sony has eight from the company and seven from the outside. Nearly all companies have a lower ratio of independent directors than Sony. Japanese U.S.-style management simply means the inclusion of outsiders on the board.

Independent directors were sitting on boards in Japan years ago. For example, there have long been companies with two or three directors from banks or government. Nowadays, companies are merely making small increases in the number of outside directors they have. But directors from the company will always be in the majority. This is described as U.S.-style but it is essentially the same management style long practiced in Japan. I could probably count on the fingers of one hand the number of Japanese companies truly practicing U.S.-style management. Companies are free to choose a management style. If U.S.-style management suits a company, so be it.

THE SIGNIFICANCE OF LIFETIME EMPLOYMENT

Q: *Against the background of a reported collapse of the lifetime-employment system in Japan, your call for its continuation has raised eyebrows.*

A: Canon is regarded as unusual in that it offers lifetime employment, but lifetime employment has been common in Japan. It is often said that the labor market in Japan is growing more mobile. But I have lived in both the U.S. and Japan, and in comparison with the U.S., Japan is not yet a mobile society.

Canon has never had an external director in the 66 years since its establishment and it is upholding that tradition. The reason is that we don't want to squash employees' dreams. At Canon, an employee becomes eligible for a directorship after 30 years of service. A directorship is a goal toward which all employees can strive. Therefore, Canon has observed a policy of not allowing outsiders to deprive employees of that opportunity.

Canon limits the number of directors to 30. However, there have never been 30 directors. There are always two or three vacancies on the board to accommodate outstanding employees. At Canon we maintain relationships of trust between employees. Because employees work hard in hopes of becoming a director, they have an exceedingly keen interest in internal checks. This is a Canon tradition. It is in itself, I believe, a rational mechanism. Rationalism is doing what's necessary, as circumstances demand.

Q: *Does Canon give weight to promotions from within, in contrast to U.S. companies, where the trend is to introduce more people from the outside?*

A: Japanese management does not have an accurate understanding of the U.S. system. In contrast to the general perception, most CEOs of top U.S. companies have risen from within their organizations. That is a fact.

American society is definitely marked by high mobility. Americans are ambitious and rise to challenges. Therefore, in the U.S., the cream of the crop compete inside the company and outside the company. If their job performance is inadequate, there is a chance they will be replaced by talented people from outside the company. The person who wins the competition against his peers and outsiders and rises to CEO is a superior individual.

Even in America a lot of people spend many years working for a single company because their employment is a source of pride. So, in effect, they have lifetime employment. The person who can work for years despite the constant fear of being replaced is superior. Therefore, even the mail clerk takes pride in maintaining his position as a mail clerk through his working life. When such a person retires, his colleagues hold a party for him at the company.

In my opinion, in America external directors rarely perform a management supervisory function. However, I do think they are significant as sources of ideas and do perform a consulting function. But at other companies, CEOs and directors are often fired or replaced — which I think hurts a company's performance. The CEO and directors are selected and brought from outside the company on the basis of capacity, career and compensation. No one knows much about their character. If that's the case, then it is only natural someone outside the company must evaluate them. At a company with a high turnover of personnel, a check mechanism must, of course, be in place. If the CEO and directors are hired through headhunters, in which case the company doesn't know what sort of people it is getting, the check mechanism and oversight must be performed externally.

It seems to me that Japanese companies are using this type of U.S. company — rather than the top U.S. companies I spoke of earlier — as their model. Even in America, a company with revolving-door directors is not a top company. I don't understand why the Japanese are so eager to imitate such a phenomenon.

But what is the situation at Japanese companies? In Japan, people whose characters are not well known don't become directors. Because only employees who have earned trust after 20 or 30 years of inhouse evaluation become directors, there is no need for oversight and supervision by an evaluation mechanism comprising mainly outsiders. For example, I make directors people with whom I've worked for many years. If I were to bring people from the outside to evaluate and supervise them, I would lose the trust of our directors. That would be foolish.

Such an evaluation mechanism is not necessary in a society built on trust, such as in Japan. Japanese companies would be better devoting themselves to creating an organization free of failures and accounting irregularities. A mechanism for the supervision of directors is nowhere near as necessary in Japan as it is in the U.S.

But I'm often told that scandals involving directors are a reality anywhere in the world. However, scandals will occur whether companies adopt the Japanese or American model of management. They are unavoidable. They are to be expected. You should not expect the U.S. management model, with its external check mechanism, to make any difference. After all, don't incidents occur even in America where the check mechanism is in place?

WILL JAPAN'S CORPORATE CULTURE CHANGE?

Q: *You have said a community spirit, like the one that existed in feudal domains during Japan's Edo Period, remains strong in Japanese corporate culture; and that this spirit has supported the sort of Japanese style of management you have been describing. But don't you feel that the Japanese will come to have an attitude similar to Americans, who live in a highly mobile society?*

A: I don't think the Japanese attitude will change greatly. Nor do I think it necessary to force it to change.

A true citizen of the world is not stateless. So, for example, we can speak of world citizens of Japanese origin or of

U.S. origin, meaning world citizens who are Japanese or world citizens who are American. There is, for instance, a world citizen of U.S. origin in Canon's public relations department. He is a well-educated man raised in the U.S. He is an outstanding American. He came to Japan and understands the country such that he fits in and lives in the Japanese way. If he returns to the U.S., he can live in the American way. He is what I call a world citizen.

I myself live in Japan as a Japanese but have the experience of long residence in the U.S., and, because I can understand America's culture, I can behave as an American in the United States. And back in Japan I act as a Japanese.

You possess traits that are part of your nature. Your culture is often an innate part of your personality. On that basis, if you acquire the culture of a foreign country such that you can behave as one of its people when you visit it, you are a world citizen. Against the background of globalization, the need for such people will increase.

World citizenship is desirable for both the individual and the company. That is why I manage the company from the perspective of a world citizen. It is my fundamental principle.

A Japanese company, even one described as a global one, should not become a U.S. company in Japan. Do you think IBM's Japanese operation is managed in a U.S. style? In practice it is not. It is to a large degree run in the Japanese way. Whether speaking of an individual or a company, the Japanese way is fine. Why? Say a Japanese went to the U.S. and suggested instituting Japanese-style lifetime employment. Everyone would think he was odd. Before he knew it, every last capable employee would have quit. Conversely, if someone in Japan began firing people right and left as in America, no replacements would come. Japan doesn't have a mobile labor market.

A style that fits the country, embracing its accepted ways — these are the prerequisites for being a global company. Without doubt, a culture changes little by little. As it evolves, a company's management and an individual's outlook on life will also change. But I think Japanese scholars and pundits contradict themselves. In my experience, if you compare Japan and the U.S., the former has not yet achieved the latter's level of labor mobility. Despite that, pundits speak as if it has. That really irks me.

Q: *In many cases, the domination of management by people who have risen through the ranks causes them to think only of the interests of the company, and not necessarily those of society at large. What measures do you take to ensure that Canon's management acts in the best interests of the company and society?*

A: I take three measures. The first is giving Canon employees moral education every year. We have a code of ethics for employees. We instill in employees from the start of their careers that society's interests take precedence over the company's interests. I personally give lectures to company executives. These lectures have been gathered into an anthology for employees.

Another measure is the establishment of a management supervision group under direct presidential control. This is in addition to auditors. This team comprises 20 inspectors with expertise in accounting and other areas. They routinely examine the various departments' expense sheets for irregularities. They examine all departments, from development to production and sales, and, of course, they conduct examinations without prior appointment. Thus there is always exhaustive internal supervision. This inspection team helps to prevent fraud.

The third measure is always to deepen communication. Directors participate daily in a morning meeting. This meeting is off the record and any topic is okay. It is a forum for free exchange. Often the topic is a scandal at another company, and the directors will discuss what should not be done at Canon. People can't do anything wrong if they get together for an exchange like our morning meetings.

To be frank, the frequent exchange of opinions at the morning meetings becomes corporate governance and is related to the propagation of compliance. Someone who has done something wrong doesn't put on a good face in the morning. Our corporate governance consists of frank board meetings and a high degree of transparency. Corporate governance is not just a matter of external checks; rather, in a broad sense, it is internal corporate governance. It is, broadly speaking, culture — a combination of the employees' spirit of compliance and company spirit. The spirit of compliance wed to company spirit belongs to one category of corporate governance.

All the same, it's necessary to let sunshine into a company. In that respect, we are bringing the talents of outside advisors inside the company. For example, in 2002 we inaugurated an inhouse training program that employed such advisors to help train employees to become directors. Hitotsubashi University's Professor Shinichiro Yonekura led the team of more than 10 external instructors, which included Tokyo University's Professor Ken Sakamura. The instructors taught from morning to evening on Saturdays for seven months. They drilled the potential directors in everything from ethics to politics and education. No one cut class. We provided that sort of education and made four of the students directors.

Q: *But who will watch the directors? Under the system of internal promotion, those chosen by the person at the top may not be best suited to do the watching. In such a case, wouldn't it be better to have a director from outside the company?*

A: That is unrealistic. Even someone from outside the company would not be able to monitor directors. He would have more difficulty than a person inside the company. It is hard to stop abuse, in any event. There is perhaps no company anywhere that, over the long run, can escape having a top executive who abuses his post.

Q: *There is also the example of Louis V. Gerstner, who came to IBM from the outside and revitalized the company.*

A: He is an exception. In IBM's long history, he is the only person who has come into the company from outside. Consider General Electric. During a history spanning more than 100 years, not a single General Electric CEO has come from outside the company. Certainly every company will face a crisis once every few decades. However, it is inefficient to institute measures to prepare for such a crisis. Rather, it is best not to even contemplate such measures.

Q: *In your vision of Canon as a global company, how do you view the respective roles of the Japanese headquarters, your U.S. operations and your European operations?*

A: First of all, I want Canon's overseas companies to be world class in their countries. Canon has 14,000 U.S. employees, and sales have reached ¥1 trillion in the U.S. But the configuration whereby Canon U.S.A. imports products from Japan, sells them, and realizes a margin is not an efficient use of capital. The company should increasingly shift to manufacturing. I want the company to make and sell products globally that are different from Canon Japan's. It can sell them in America and export them to Japan. The same holds true for Canon Europe.

Earlier, I said something to the effect that an individual or a company must blend into the host country while preserving their own identity. I want Canon U.S.A. to be a top company in America. I want Canon Japan to be a leading company in Japan and the rest of Asia. If we balanced the books on a consolidated basis, we could minimize exchange-rate fluctuations — the biggest problem we face. This is my dream for an ideal management configuration, although I'm not sure how many decades it will take for this to be realized.

Q: *How close are you to that goal?*

A: I've still got a long way to go. Not everyone is prepared for the challenge. A goal of this magnitude requires patience. But if we chart the right course, we will achieve the goal someday. Because we have charted a course and have committed, talented people, I think we will achieve the ideal configuration.

STRATEGY FOR CHINA

Q: *China is attracting attention as a market. American and European companies also want a share of the Chinese market.*

Against growing competition, how does Canon intend to increase its share of the Chinese market?

A: We began by investing heavily in China as a manufacturing base, and that investment is now paying off. China now accounts for about 20% of production for the Canon group overall. That is a great help. Now that the dust has settled from plant investment, production is steadily increasing.

Now we are investing in sales. We established Canon China with headquarters in Beijing, and sent executives and directors from Japan. We aim to create 15 branch offices throughout China. Ten branches have already been opened.

China is an attractive market of immense scale. In the future it would be ideal to develop products in China for the Chinese market, and to manufacture and sell them there. With its entry into the World Trade Organization, over the next five or 10 years China will gradually liberalize its market. We will invest in our sales and service networks in pace with its market liberalization. We are implementing that plan now.

China is industrializing. Its middle class is growing. Japanese companies are eager to play a part in China's industrialization and look forward to the future.

Q: *What are your stratagems for winning the competition against other makers?*

A: In the age of globalization, a company must win everywhere. Therefore, if it wins in Japan, it also wins overseas. It can't win in Japan but lose in China. In order to win, a company must differentiate its products everywhere. The entire world is a single market in the age of globalization. Because we are doing roughly the same things in China and Japan, if we win in the latter, we should also win in the former.

Q: *China is inundated with imitation products.*

A: I strongly wish the Chinese would stop manufacturing counterfeit products. Because the Chinese government appears to be clamping down on counterfeits, I expect the problem will gradually subside. I hope the Chinese government continues in this campaign. That would be in China's national interest because, after all, in the global marketplace under the WTO system, brands will also emerge from Chinese products in the future.

Q: *Have you dispatched personnel from the head office's intellectual-property section to China?*

A: Two intellectual-property specialists are combating imitation products in China. They have detected a large number of imitation products. The Chinese government has been very cooperative. When the two specialists find imitation products, they inform the authorities. Of course, there are more than two working to root out imitation products. The two specialists have employed many Chinese assistants, with whom they work as teams.

PRODUCTION INNOVATION

Q: *Competition is heating up in markets for digital cameras and other products. What is the outlook for these?*

A: Not in a thousand years will there ever be markets or products without competition. The only answer is to make a winning product. Today I'm concentrating on cost reduction through integration of development and production, and product differentiation. Some say that because we have already completed the conversion to the cell method at all our factories, innovation is over and nothing remains to be done. That's a ridiculous comment. There is still much to do. We are only half done.

Our never-ending challenge is to make Canon a company immune to the effects of exchange-rate fluctuations in an age of globalization. Therefore, it is important is to reduce production costs. If we reduce production costs, and our margin increases, the company can withstand small exchange-rate fluctuations. Thus, we must cut production costs.

So far, I have changed the production system and the development system. Next, I'll address the challenge of cost reduction through integration of development and production.

To that end, I must first increase the speed of development. We have already introduced 3D computer-aided design (CAD) for all our designs. Ultimately, if development can be completed through 3D CAD, we can begin mass production much faster and cut costs drastically. Production prototypes are very expensive. We can prepare for production at the plant while we do the design by 3D CAD. Until now, we have drawn a plan, done the design by two-dimensional CAD, made a working prototype and evaluated a production version. If there was a problem, we redrew the plan and made another working prototype. We repeated this process until we came up with a sound production version.

This approach requires a tremendous amount of time and money. We must shift to a system whereby we make the design and prototype entirely by 3D CAD, and concurrently prepare for production. If we eliminate the prototype, we save the cost of its production and can shorten the development period by the time spent in the prototype phase. This is my aim.

But we have to significantly raise the level of our system analysis technology, simulation technology and measurement technology if we are to approach this ideal. For that purpose, I'm now rapidly investing in those technologies. If we can't improve our measurement technology and fulfill all the other conditions, we will not be able to create a perfect design by 3D CAD.

If the pace of design and development pick up, two additional benefits will accrue. One is that we can avoid a price war. If a product becomes obsolete, a price war ensues. Then the profit rate drops. Therefore, before we fall into a price war, we can maintain a fixed profit rate by offering a good product with high added value for the same price.

The other benefit — an important one — is the avoidance of exchange risks. Just because the yen is strong doesn't mean we can raise the price of cameras selling in New York by the amount of the rise in the value of the currency. The reason is that the strong yen is of absolutely no concern to Americans. The yen–dollar rate is irrelevant to U.S. consumers. One dollar is one dollar. Therefore, if the strong yen raises the price of a product from US$10 to US$11, U.S. consumers will not buy it.

So what should we do? We must switch to new products that are economically viable at the current yen–dollar rate. The faster we switch to new products, the greater the efficacy against the strong yen. For the above reasons, the creation of a system of integrated development and production is important. As well, if the quality of design is good, the plant will not turn out flawed or defective products. This will also contribute to cost reduction.

Q: *Isn't that similar to upstream process control in the field of quality control?*

A: Yes, it's upstream process control. Therefore, cost reduction is necessary from the development stage. Of course, we must devise a more rational production system through, for example, the introduction of robots into the cell method, the combination of humans and robots, or completely automated factories. Such measures would drive down production costs further in Japan.

Q: *The emphasis on continual cost reduction resembles the thinking at Toyota.*

A: Toyota is about 10 years ahead of us. If a Toyota person overheard me, he might laugh, because they have already thought about this.

Q: *At Toyota, if a problem is identified, they make repeated assessments until they have the solution.*

A: I've also imitated Toyota in this regard. At the work site, a problem should be thoroughly pursued until a solution is found. Until the solution is reflected in business figures, I go to the site and implement action. That is normal.

Q: *But it must be difficult to implant that way of thinking company wide.*

A: Yes, it has to be made part of the culture. I'm doing that. Other managers have done the same thing. But in the history of Canon I'm perhaps the first to do so.

LONG-RANGE PLANNING

Q: *You revised upwards the target figures for the second phase of your long-term plan, a five-year plan that began in 2001, which succeeds the first five-year plan begun in 1996. What is the outlook for achieving those targets?*

A: Because we achieved our target for profits two years ahead of schedule, we revised our targets slightly upward. Profit for the current term, the third quarter, already surpasses profit for the previous term. Therefore, we will achieve our five-year plan targets without difficulty.

Because we forecast the achievement of those targets, from this year we began preparations for the third phase of the long-term planning, which will span five years beginning in 2006. We are already taking steps to ensure this plan succeeds.

This third phase will raise Canon's science and technology to a higher level in order to increase high added value. How will we achieve that? Let me mention one already visible step. We rebuilt our headquarters building and have begun the design of a high-tech research institute. The institute will be built on our head office grounds and be five stories above ground and three below ground, with a total area of 40,000 square meters. It will house a research and development facility that will consolidate Canon's core technology expertise. We will relocate our central laboratory there from Atsugi (about 50 kilometers southwest of Tokyo) to create a major research and development center.

Also, we have bought land near our head office. On that plot we will gather together all our scattered printer-related facilities and build a materials research laboratory. It will be the workplace of the printer-development team and of the team doing research in inkjet-related inks and other materials.

Furthermore, we are building in Utsunomiya (about 100 kilometers north of Tokyo) a second optics research laboratory and a plant for the flat-panel SED display we are developing in cooperation with Toshiba. We have decided to build a second camera-assembly plant and are now preparing the ground at the site. This plant will not simply be a place for mass production, but will also provide generous space for basic research and technology research for cameras.

This sort of investment should bear fruit during the third phase, raising the level of our R&D and technology such that our cameras, printers, and other existing products are the best in the world. Also, we will be making our full-fledged entry into SED and other new fields.

The infrastructure of which I've been speaking will be completed by 2005 or early 2006. By achieving second-phase targets ahead of schedule, we have planted the seeds for early success in the third phase. Now that we have finished planting the seeds, we have begun watering them. We will definitely move forward.

Q: *So Canon will continue to forge ahead?*

A: I'm not the type who thinks, "If I reach this point, I can take it easy." Because we have adopted a merit-based pay system, employees who perform well are amply rewarded. Those with poor track records see little rise in their compensation. I'll be honest with you, we're in good shape. That's why everyone is working in high spirits. I, too, am working hard. Thoughts of taking it easy never cross my mind.

THE ROLE OF EDUCATION

Q: *It is argued that education is the key to reviving corporate Japan. How should Japan nurture its human resources?*

A: The reality is that academic performance has declined in Japanese grade schools and middle schools. Because Japan has no natural resources and depends for its survival on creating added value through industrialization, the decline in performance, a basic source of strength, is a dangerous trend.

Moreover, Japan has not clarified its national values during the long period since the end of World War II. Schools are not imparting a solid education. There is still confusion about whether schools can fly the national flag and students can sing the national anthem. This situation must be rectified.

If you begin to speak of national values, you fall into a debate about militarism, which is why many Japanese skirt the issue today. Harmonious existence is a Canon principle. We have as a principle the harmonious existence of humankind. In that sense, we should educate our children on the basis of a solid self-awareness as Japanese. We should educate them in such a way that while possessing a sense of national identity, they can get along with other peoples in the age of globalization. I think that is the fundamental education for a world citizen.

Q: *What can Canon do? What must Canon do?*

A: Canon is involved with education in the area of cooperation between industry and academia. It is little concerned with education itself. What I said earlier was very much my own opinion. I would like to add that in order for the Japanese to exist as members of the international community, they must be good Japanese even before they are world citizens.

THE FORMATION OF MITARAI'S CHARACTER

Q: *What was the biggest influence on the formation of your character?*

A: The environment of my childhood home. My father, a physician, was very strict. Both my parents had a fervor for education. We were an old family. It was our tradition to concern ourselves with the welfare of the entire town and with the welfare of society, and to emphasize contributions to society. My family stretches back 16 generations. It has been contributing to the development of the town for generations. My father was industrious, austere and education-minded. I observed his attitude toward people in his capacity as a physician, and as a town and community leader. It was my observation of him that formed my character. I only lived at home until age 15. But both of my parents lived past my 50th birthday. My family had a big influence on me.

I was raised in comfortable circumstances but because my parents were strict, I don't recall being pampered. We didn't indulge in luxury. The home of my elder brother, a physician in the family tradition, is like that even today.

I think the rigor of my approach to business is a result of the influence of having spent 23 years as a businessman in competitive U.S. society. And yet, at the same time, I like the atmosphere at Canon and I advocate the meritocratic system and lifetime employment because of the influence of the company's founder. As CEO, I will continue to uphold Canon's traditions. I believe it is my mission to develop the company in a form suited to the times.

Epilogue From the Japanese Edition

In October 2001, when Jack Welch, former chairman of General Electric, addressed the Global Management Forum (sponsored by the business daily *Nihon Keizai Shimbun*), he suggested that Canon and Toyota were points of reference for the reform of Japan's corporations. This comment was made as this book was being completed, and Welch's remark was not incorporated in the text, but at the time we strongly felt that our own thinking differed little from his.

There's no panacea for corporate reform. There's no easy prescription on the order of, "Take this and get well." What has to be done, however, is to continually take into account many factors, such as a company's vision, its history, its present situation, its competitors and its "physical condition." One must proceed, flexibly, with an open mind and execute the optimum combination of strategies for a company. In a continually unfolding process, it is dynamism in particular that represents a source of strength. Although this advice may appear quite obvious, we would be contented if readers learn only this lesson from this book.

In writing this book, interviews that had been published in the *Nihon Keizai Shimbun*, and a series that ran in the *Nikkei Sangyo Shimbun* were used; almost all of the material was completely rewritten. While we referred to a wide range of source material, we found the following of particular assistance:

Ryuzaburo Kaku, "My Personal History" (Watashi no Rirekisho), *Nihon Keizai Shimbun*, March 1993

A Posthumous Biography of Takeshi Mitarai (Miyakozo Yayoino – Mitarai Takeshi Tsuitoushu), privately published

Fifty Year History of Canon – Its Technology and Products (Canon-shi, Gijutsu to Seihin no Gojunen), privately published

Canon Life, Sixtieth Anniversary Edition (Canon Life, Kaisha Soritsu Rokuju-Shunen Kinengo), privately published

Outrunning a Dream – Takeshi Mitarai and the Canon Company (Yume ga Kakenuketa – Mitarai Takeshi to Canon), Gendai Sozo Sha

The writing was done primarily by Kiyoshi Tokuda and Yoshinori Omura of the Editorial Bureau of the *Nihon Keizai Shimbun*.

In the course of preparing the text, much valuable information was obtained and we are grateful for the help of those interviewed at Canon—the CEO, officers, employees, and former employees. They are too many to identify by name, but we thank every one of them. We owe a debt of gratitude especially to Ryoichi Sawaai, Bunji Yano, and Richard Berger of the Corporate Communications Headquarters at Canon, for their help in responding to a stream of our requests for information.

November 2001

Index